SUBURBIA
The American Dream and Dilemma

PHILIP C. DOLCE is Associate Professor of History and Co-ordinator of Public Media Programming at Bergen Community College. He received his Ph.D. from Fordham University. Dr. Dolce coedited *Cities in Transition: From the Ancient World to Urban America* and *Power and the Presidency*. An Associate of the Columbia University Seminar on the City, his articles have appeared in a number of books and journals. He has produced many radio and television programs including: the CBS television series "Science and Society: A Humanistic View," and "The Transformation of American Society," the WPAT radio series "Higher Education in America," and the NBC television series "The American Suburbs: Myth and Reality." Dr. Dolce founded the Media Instructional Association and presently serves as its director.

SUBURBIA

The American Dream and Dilemma

EDITED BY PHILIP C. DOLCE

ANCHOR BOOKS

ANCHOR PRESS/DOUBLEDAY

GARDEN CITY, NEW YORK

1976

LIBRARY OF CONGRESS CATALOGING IN PUBLICATION DATA
MAIN ENTRY UNDER TITLE:
SUBURBIA: THE AMERICAN DREAM AND DILEMMA.
INCLUDES BIBLIOGRAPHICAL REFERENCES AND INDEX.
1. SUBURBS—UNITED STATES—ADDRESSES, ESSAYS, LECTURES. I.
DOLCE, PHILIP C.
HT123.s788   301.36′2′0973

THE ANCHOR PRESS EDITION IS THE FIRST PUBLICATION OF
SUBURBIA: THE AMERICAN DREAM AND DILEMMA.

ANCHOR BOOKS EDITION: 1976
ISBN: 0-385-01336-1
LIBRARY OF CONGRESS CATALOG CARD NUMBER 76-2838

To Susan's grandparents,

Joseph and Emma Dolce and
Frank and Antoinette Pasciuto

CONTENTS

PREFACE

SUBURBIA, THE MIDDLE GROUND between nature's beauty and civilization's conveniences, has been viewed as the promised land by millions of Americans over the last several generations. Traditionally, the dream of a single-family detached house in a safe, homogeneous setting, which would foster a renewed sense of family life, was so strong that it literally transformed the American landscape. While many families were seeking this private vision in the suburbs, others also saw the middle landscape as a promised land for quite different reasons. Some reformers and planners believed that suburbia would alleviate the problems of major cities by providing a safety valve for excessive population and social problems. Others hoped to create entirely new community forms in America's last frontier.

Each special vision of suburbia was developed without adequate recognition that the people who settled in the new landscape would carry traditional class and ethnic values with them. The dreams also would be altered by the financial ability of each group to pay for them. The private vision of most Americans conflicted with the social goals planners and reformers hoped to attain in suburbia. Moreover, suburbs were not developed in a void but rather reflected the entrepreneurial skills of builders and land speculators as did American cities and rural areas in an earlier period. Finally, the middle landscape is a child of affluence and efficiency was never one of its birthrights.

The result of multiple visions, traditional values, haphazard government intervention and technological innovations, working within a capitalistic system, is seen in the tremendous variation of communities found within the middle landscape. There are working-class suburbs, elite suburbs, black suburbs, ethnic suburbs, industrial suburbs, and planned suburbs among others. Suburbia today is a reflection of America's pluralistic and segmented society.

While it is evident that suburbia is not monolithic and has not created a special social character for Americans, there is a desperate need to believe it has. As Bennett Berger and others have observed, builders and speculators helped to create a homogeneous image in order to market and sell suburbia to the public. The myth of suburban life was sustained by a variety of groups for a number of different reasons. For some it covered over the diversity of American culture and affirmed that there was "an American Way of Life" which all citizens proudly could aspire to. Those who were dissatisfied with some aspect of our society also found the myth of suburbia useful to attack a wide variety of national problems ranging from social conformity to ecology.

Despite the unrealistic boosterism and criticism, many people have derived some satisfaction from suburban life. Judging by those already living there and the countless numbers who would, if finances and discriminatory ordinances permitted, suburbia can provide a livable, if not perfect, environment. More importantly, suburban development has had a major impact on the nation. The fact that millions of Americans sought to fulfill their dreams in the middle landscape has caused a national dilemma, especially for our cities. For the first time in our history, or in the history of any nation, more people now live in suburbs than in central cities or rural areas. The disparity in population statistics becomes even greater when one considers that suburbs now contain over 55 per cent of the metropolitan area population in the nation. In terms of affluence, American suburbs are the residential areas for an overwhelming proportion of the college trained, those engaged in professional pursuits, and of all families in the upper-income brackets. The cities with less than 45 per cent of the metropolitan area population now contain over half the poor, unskilled, and aged portion of the population in these regions. In addition, suburban areas now have as many jobs as cities and will probably exceed the employment opportunities of urban centers in the near future.

The aim of this volume is to view the development of suburbia, examine certain aspects of the life-style found there, and understand the impact it has had on the nation. Since the study of suburbia transcends any one discipline, we have attempted to combine the expertise and perspectives of historians, political scientists, artists, urban planners, and suburban reformers in order to present the reader with a multidimensional view. In doing so, there has been no attempt to impose a particular thesis on all the articles or reconcile contrasting interpretations presented by the contributors. Naturally, limitations of space and the fact that the volume is primarily intended for students and general readers forced a certain degree of selectivity in the topics chosen to be covered in these essays.

I would like to express my sincere appreciation to all contributors for their participation in this project; they deserve full credit for the merits of this volume. Marie Brown of Doubleday was a source of constant encouragement and her patience and understanding will always be appreciated. A very special note of gratitude belongs to Mary Christiano and Mary Darragh, my colleagues at Bergen Community College, who provided indispensable assistance in the preparation of this manuscript. The volume is dedicated to my daughter's grandparents as a small token of our love and affection. Of course, my wife, Patty, and daughter, Susan, helped by just being part of my life.

PHILIP C. DOLCE

CONTRIBUTORS

MARY E. BROOKS is Director of Research at the Suburban Action Institute. She received her M.A. in City and Regional Planning from Ohio State University and is the author of a forthcoming book on housing rights and the environment. Ms. Brooks's numerous articles and reports have been issued by many organizations including the American Society of Planning Officials.

STANLEY BUDER is Associate Professor of History and Chairman of the Department at Bernard Baruch College of the City University of New York. He received his Ph.D. from the University of Chicago and is the author of *Pullman: An Experiment in Industrial Order and Community Planning* and *Ebenezer Howard and the Rise of the Garden City Movement*. Dr. Buder's articles have appeared in the *Journal of the American Institute of Planners, American Biographical Dictionary*, and the *Encyclopedia of Town and City Planning*. He is an Associate of the Columbia University Seminar on the City and was a consultant to the Chicago Historical Landmark Commission.

FRANK J. COPPA is Associate Professor of History at St. John's University. He received his Ph.D. from Catholic University of America. Dr. Coppa is the author of *Planning, Protectionism and Politics in Liberal Italy* and *Camillo di Cavour;* coeditor of *Cities in Transition: From the Ancient World to Urban America, The Immigrant in American Life*, and *From Vienna to Vietnam, War and Peace in the Modern*

World; and editor of *Religion in the Making of Western Man.* An Associate of the Columbia University Seminar on Modern Italy, Dr. Coppa's articles have appeared in many books and journals including the *Journal of Economic History,* the *Journal of Modern History,* and the *Journal of Church and State.*

PAUL DAVIDOFF is Director of the Suburban Action Institute. He received his M.A. in City Planning and LL.B. from the University of Pennsylvania. Mr. Davidoff's articles have appeared in many popular and learned journals including the *Journal of the American Institute of Planners, Syracuse Law Review,* and the New York *Times Magazine.* He served as a consultant to the National Commission on Urban Problems, the New York City Planning Commission, the Philadelphia Housing Association, the United States Civil Rights Commission, and many other organizations. Mr. Davidoff was the Director of the Urban Research Center at Hunter College and a member of the Board of Governors of the American Institute of Planners.

KENNETH T. JACKSON is Professor of History at Columbia University and Director of the Columbia College Urban Studies Program. He received his Ph.D. from the University of Chicago and is the author of *The Ku Klux Klan in the City, 1915–1930,* and coeditor of *American Vistas,* and *Cities in American History.* Dr. Jackson's articles have appeared in many books and learned journals. He is Executive Secretary of the Society of American Historians, Senior Associate of the New York Urban Coalition, and a consultant to the Metropolitan Applied Research Center. Dr. Jackson founded the Columbia University Seminar on the City and served as its chairman.

SAMUEL KAPLAN is Director of Development of the New York City Educational Construction Fund and Adjunct Professor at the School of Architecture and Environmental Studies of the City College of New York. Mr. Kaplan received his education at Cornell University. He is the author of *The Dream Deferred: People, Politics and Planning in Suburbia* and *6:13* (a novel) and coauthor of *The New York City Handbook*. A member of the Board of *Architecture Plus*, Mr. Kaplan's work has appeared in that magazine and a number of other publications, including the New York *Times*, *Harper's*, *New York* magazine, and *City*.

MARGARET S. MARSH is Assistant Professor of Historical Studies at Stockton State College. She received her Ph.D. from Rutgers University and her work has appeared in the *Richmond Historian*.

JOEL SCHWARTZ is Assistant Professor of History at Montclair State College. He received his Ph.D. from the University of Chicago and is an Associate of the Columbia University Seminar on the City. Dr. Schwartz's work has appeared in *New York History*.

CONSTANTINE G. VASILIADIS is a consultant to state and community arts organizations and is currently Director of Audience Development for the New Jersey Symphony. He received his education at Yale University and the Juilliard School of Music. Mr. Vasiliadis formerly served as Executive Director of the North Jersey Cultural Council and as a co-ordinator of the theater grant program of the New York State Council on the Arts. He also served as Public Relations Director of the Brooklyn Academy of Music and as Assistant Director of Education at the Lincoln Center for the Performing Arts. While at Lincoln Center, Mr. Vasiliadis was educational advisor to the New York Philharmonic, the New York City Ballet, the Metropolitan Opera Studio, and the Juilliard School of Music.

PIERCE B. WILKINSON is Associate Professor of Political Science at Bergen Community College. He received his education at Fordham and New York universities. Professor Wilkinson has appeared on a number of radio and television programs dealing with contemporary political problems.

EVOLUTION OF THE SUBURBS
by Joel Schwartz

SUBURBS PRESENT a special challenge to the American historian. The remarkable metropolitan growth of the last quarter century climaxed by the startling 1970 census which declared America a suburban nation makes urgent an understanding of the origins and parameters of this development. Regrettably, historians have not easily related to this field. Scholars accustomed to the slow accretion of institutional artifacts find "suburbia" an overnight wonder on a thousand housing tracts, bulldozed of all "history" save the crabbed antiquarian who recalls established families overrun by "the newcomers." Yet the history of suburban America reaches back one hundred and thirty years. For at least that long, urban dwellers have tried to escape the city's grime, immigrants, and disorder and searched for outlying retreats with institutional structures to protect their preserves when distance alone did not suffice. The first recognizable outward movement occurred during the social upheaval of the age of Jackson. Before World War I a distinct suburban consciousness emerged which, building upon a tradition of insular politics, utilized the latest techniques of regional planning and zoning. "Ticky-tacky" houses, shopping centers, and even auto expressways, all synonymous with mass suburbia of the late 1940s, made their impact on the metropolitan landscape before the 1929 crash. But at the most intimate level, records of countless communities reveal the extent to which the euphemism "metropolitan growth" has obscured those class and ethnic conflicts deflected to the city's periphery. The American metropolis has been a seamless web of migratory peoples and institutions, with suburbs sharing more than they have cared to admit of the ways of life of the inner city.

Traditionally, "suburbs" have been the haunts of the poor on land not yet taken up by the rich. In "preindustrial" cities across the globe, established caste groups clung to the civic centers where palace, cathedral, and guild hall dispensed wealth and prestige. The less affluent found lodging where they might, while the poor and outcast huddled beyond the walls, whether London's Cheapside or Paris' swamp, the Marais. American communities up to the 1850s took much the same form. Wealthy merchants built town houses on expensive real estate around the central commons, leaving the poor, free blacks, and a growing number of Irish to crowd in jerry-built shelters on cheaper outlying lots. Had the nation possessed a different social ethic which emphasized rigid corporate structures, its cities might have preserved this traditionalism, much like the staunch caste lines, bolstered by a *conquistador* mentality, which still keep Indians, mixbloods, and Bantus beyond the pale in Mexico City and Johannesburg. But in America, urban wealth and privilege has proved vulnerable to a commercial utilitarianism which reckoned everything by an impersonal calculus. Attempts at social control, whether a Puritan sense of commonweal, the voluntary night watch, or walled private blocks, were overwhelmed by the upheaval of the nineteenth century.

As a consequence, suburban communities formed from a largely middle-class migration reflected a peculiar ambivalence toward downtown. While they bought homes on the fringe to escape factories, immigrants, and Negroes, the middle class remained tied to umbilical commuter routes, habituated to urban consumer standards and to a thousand delights which only downtown could provide. The suburbanite sought a pastoral retreat which was paved, electrified, and serviced by trained professionals. He dreamed of a private garden spot, but one never far removed from the easy camaraderie enjoyed back in the city. The homeowner sought to preserve his beloved ground by sheer distance and a welter of restrictive covenants, but found that community solidarity crumbled when offered tempting real estate profits. Because of this vulnerability, the suburbanization of America has meant more than physical removal beyond the built-up portions of the city; it has also included a pervasive yearning, often frustrated by an individualistic ethos, for some sense of attachment to a covenanted community.

SUBURBAN ORIGINS: THE PROTESTANT CITY IN TRANSITION

In colonial America, urban elites, repelled by the growing disorder of their seaports yet drawn by their commercial vigor, found it difficult to leave their cities completely. Boston's merchants who moved to Dorchester Neck and Roxbury in the 1720s and Manhattan aristocrats who built mansions in Harlem village before the Revolution sought seasonal escape from dreaded yellow fever while enjoying the villa existence of the semiretired. As long as the primitive division of labor required personal supervision of industry, active merchants maintained in-town residences and usually lived above their workshops. Street life and pageantry also exerted an undeniable pull. The ambitious, personable man of "affairs," like Benjamin Franklin, found much to engage his interest: church vestries, fire companies, militia troops, Fourth of July parades, Bunker Hill celebrations, and civic festivals of all kinds.

The first large-scale suburban migration coincided with the industrialization and immigration which transformed city life before the Civil War. Steam hammers drowned out church bells, railroad viaducts tore through established neighborhoods, and coal soot drifted down everywhere. After the 1837 panic, hard times aggravated the shift from handicraft to factory employment. German and Irish immigrants swamped the cities in the 1840s. Their Popish rites offended staid Protestants and their fire "laddies" collided with Protestant associations in the streets. Ethnic tensions coupled with sharper job competition set off nativist riots that scarred the next decade. While ministers exhorted a return to Sunday pieties, commercial elites invigorated police forces, militia commands, and lockups. The rich began to seek asylum in Beacon Hill or Girard Row, exclusive neighborhoods with restrictive covenants and a social hauteur that kept out interlopers. Few of these enclaves went as far as the private "places" of St. Louis' West Side, controlled by propertyowners' associations, surrounded by gates, and patrolled by hired guards. For the time being, stout granite walls along with platooned police served to keep the city's chaos at a distance.

The intellectual spirit of the Jacksonian age, however, was convinced that only total removal to the countryside would suffice. Sharing Jefferson's suspicion of cities, inspired by European Romantic musings, and, above all, unnerved by the preternatural growth of New York and Boston, a generation of writers from Thoreau to William Cullen Bryant searched for God's immanent presence in the country. Ante-bellum reformers also believed that urban poverty and vice could be eliminated by egalitarian and harmonious villages built afresh outside the cities. Fourierites like Parke Godwin urged the planting of factories in the fields and encouraged workingmen's advocates to include "land reform" among their legislative proposals. To uplift the harried urban gentry, landscape architects Andrew Jackson Downing and Calvert Vaux designed Greek Revival cottages in leafy groves, which also proved ideal backdrops for the sentimental novelists determined to place Woman on her pedestal. Horace Greeley, Manhattan's rural cultivator, temperance advocate, and dabbler in Utopian socialism and a hundred other nostrums, summed up the era's faith in the country:

> Secure to the family the inducements of a home, surrounded by fruits and flowers, rational village movements and sports, the means of education and independence. Get them out of the cities and would-be cities into scenes like those, and the work is done.

Dreams turned to reality when a fundamental revolution in urban transportation made a long-distance commute feasible for thousands. By the 1820s, paddle steamers churned along the East River, transforming village Brooklyn into Manhattan's bedroom suburb, while Hoboken, Jersey City, and Staten Island swelled with waterborne commuters. The year of Andrew Jackson's inauguration saw the start of hack service between downtown Boston and Dorchester Neck. By the 1850s, "White Line" omnibuses offered six-cent trips between this South Boston suburb and "The Hub" every five minutes. Expensive fares still limited travel to merchants and professionals. But when the omnibus switched to rails, enabling horse teams to drag much longer coach bodies, the resulting economies ushered in an era of relative "mass" transit. Horsecars received franchises in the eastern cities by the early 1850s. During 1860, Boston's horse railways moved 13 million passengers, while Manhattan's carried a phenomenal 45 million. Now a broader sector of the community, including middle-class clerks and skilled artisans as well as bankers, could think about settling uptown. Real "rapid" transit came with steam railroads which by mid-century radiated from Boston across the Charles River and from Manhattan north across the Harlem into Westchester. The new service was not an unmitigated boon, however. For the privilege of living at greater distances from the city, these pioneer commuters paid higher fares and often endured reckless engineers, open platforms exposed to the elements, and unannounced changes in schedule. In 1859, one such "old trick" on the New York and Harlem line left a "large number of 'eight o'clockers' to make their way to the city as best they could." Dismayed, but nonetheless convinced that suburban ambience made it all worthwhile, many merchants partook of the haggard life.

The transit revolution had an immense impact on the social geography of the developing metropolis. Twenty- to fifty-cents-per-day commuting acted as a selective filter on class movement. Proprietors, master artisans, and the growing white-collar sector could afford the new technology and escape from downtown. But not so the urban masses who barely earned a dollar a day. Gradually, the horsecars and steam railroads "turned the city inside out," transforming the preindustrial landscape with its poor hoveled on the outskirts, into the modern American metropolis, with its upper-income neighborhoods segregated on the periphery. But the process seemed painfully slow to many contemporary suburbanites disconcerted by the noisome institutions which continued to exist on the urban fringe. In 1847, South Boston property owners bitterly complained that the Common Council viewed their locality as the "Botany Bay of the City, into which could be thrust those establishments which the City Fathers would consider nuisances in the neighborhood of their own private dwellings, such as Alms Houses, Prisons, and Small-pox Hospitals." The outskirts also contained powder-works, slaughterhouses, glue factories, and other pariahs barred from the central area by primitive building codes. A suburban rambler might easily stumble on one of the "model villages" over which lorded an ironmaker, piano manufacturer, or brewer inspired by some ethnic reclusiveness or Fourier whim to gather his workers around. Unsurveyed land was often dotted by the rude hovels of the immigrant poor. Irish and Germans settled "down Neck" in Newark's "Hamburg Place" at the same time a large jerry-built village of free Negroes and slaves grew on Charleston's "Neck." Through these districts ran Post Roads, plank roads, and turnpikes, often lined with saloons or more sedate wayside inns, which catered to itinerant peddlers, weary Irish dayworkers, or occasional militia companies out for a Sunday target shoot. These acres long remained the haven of gamblers, prizefighters, race touts (whether at Democratic boss John McKane's ground in Coney Island or the Chicago machine's more elegant Washington Park), camp meetings, circuses, and baseball players.

The suburban hinterland was broken up not in monotonous middle-class subdivisions, but in a kaleidoscope of settlements which reflected the full spectrum of Jacksonian community aspirations. Lowlands and highlands harbored the social extremes. By the turnpikes, behind the saloons, on the banks of streams that meandered into malarial "sloughs" squatted Irish or Negroes, trying to make a seasonal income as day laborers in nearby fields. On the hilltops lived the wealthy in pseudo-Norman castles, Italianate chateaux, or carpenter Alhambras. Cincinnati's Avondale and East Walnut Hills, Wilton in Westchester County, and West Orange outside Newark all had baronial establishments, complete with cavernous libraries, independent gas facilities, racing stables, and all else that satisfied a gentleman's taste for solitary grandeur. Far below, the industrial villages, with their planned Fourier grids, became the nucleus for German or other ethnic enclaves. Nearby, usually taking advantage of cheap horse or steam cars in the turnpike district, the moral reform societies of the 1850s, applying Greeley's advice, laid out tracts, like Pittsburgh's Temperanceville on the south side of the Monongahela, Cincinnati's Glendale, and the Westchester villages of Bronxville and Morrisania, which featured small house lots, liquor restrictions in the deeds, and specially arranged "workmen's commutation." Gradually as these subdivisions meshed together, they formed virtual extensions of the city. South Boston, Morrisania in Westchester County, and Cincinnati's Mount Auburn all were macadamized, flagged, and sidewalked, gaslit, served by horsecars, and eager for other improvements which downtown had to offer after the Civil War.

THE METROPOLITAN OUTREACH

By the second half of the nineteenth century, this disarrayed suburban patchwork sharply contrasted with the systematic expansion of the central city. The disparity fed the pervasive sense of metropolitan "manifest destiny," a conviction held by downtowners and suburbanites alike, that money, technology, and professional resources could steamroll over any difficulty. While the city reached imperialistically into its hinterland, many outlying communities proved eager to be absorbed by the new order.

Residents of the turnpike districts, painfully aware of the discrepancies between suburban shortcomings and downtown accomplishments, usually instigated the township debates for annexation to the metropolis. Aloof hilltop barons blasé about trunk sewers or macadam and local squires aghast at the thought of higher city assessments cried out against the passing of the "old-fashioned, pure democracies" which they dominated. But more middle-class voters, starved for urban amenities, determinedly carried through the referenda. Philadelphia's Northern Liberties, Spring Garden, and Kensington found by 1854 that only a metropolitan police force, free to range across municipal boundaries, could suppress street gangs which "infested" these inner suburbs. Envious of Manhattan's Croton water system and her professional police and fire departments, Morrisania and West Farms voted overwhelmingly to join New York City in 1873. Between 1867 and 1873, Boston successively annexed Roxbury, Dorchester, Brighton, and West Roxbury, suburbs that suffered lower water tables and choked on their own sewage dumped into tidal estuaries. The most startling envelopment came in 1889, when Chicago swallowed up Hyde Park township, quadrupling the city's land area and raising its population to nearly one million.

While many suburbs were a topographical chaos, garbage strewn, prey to "agues," dependent on well water and rowdy amateurs for fire protection, central cities supplied pure drinking water, "professional" police and fire departments coordinated by telegraph, and expert sanitary inspection. Between Appomattox and the 1873 depression, cities vastly increased their capital debts to splurge on spectacular improvements. At the same time, Republican party strategists had erected metropolitan districts to regulate everything from saloons and sanitation in the New York-Brooklyn area to police in Hudson County, New Jersey, to "Copperheads" in the District of Columbia. These frankly political structures, often run by city businessmen who kept metropolitan patronage in partisan hands, gave many boulevard engineers, park builders, and water-supply experts their first view of regional needs. Union Army generals, their military projects behind them, carved the outskirts into drainage districts, laid new aqueducts, and ran broad boulevards leading to park systems like Boston's Fenway and Van Courtlandt in the Bronx. More than just the source for capital improvements, the central city from 1865 to the 1890s beckoned the material well-being, professionalism, and efficiency connoted by "metropolitan" activity.

More and more this expansive spirit was epitomized by the industrial corporation whose enlarged operations built cities upward and out. During the prosperous 1880s, magnates began the search for economies of scale on the metropolitan periphery. Some sought to avoid labor radicalism, taxes, and inefficient, corrupt municipal services by building new factory towns on the cities' edges. The most celebrated of these "satellites" was Pullman, on Chicago's far South Side, where "palace" car shops sprawled with the demands of railroad logistics. The company's feudal paternalism provided workers' tenements and a central shopping arcade, but strictly barred saloons, brothels, and other unbusinesslike diversions. After the 1894 Pullman strike, however, businessmen plunged their money into factory layouts, with less concern about "amenities." The narrower outlook resulted in new communities like Gary, Indiana, which embodied "the spirit of the Corporation —efficiency." On Indiana lake-front dunes, twenty-five miles southeast of Chicago's Loop, United States Steel sited a blast-furnace complex according to the latest scientific principles. A residential quarter was platted on a strict checkerboard with back alleys reserved for utility lines, while in front the gridirons quickly filled with crowded tenements. Although Cincinnati's Oakley and Norwood contained planned industrial parks and the best railroad sites, only well-paid foremen could afford the company-built housing. Eventually, many of these working-class satellites, like Pullman, lost their "model" features and housed the saloons, commercial strips, and servant population upon which higher-class suburbs depended but preferred not to see in their midst.

In their leisure some industrialists turned to another community form equally important to the development of the metropolitan periphery, the suburban university. Although imported graduate studies may have shaped the intellectual side, higher education's physical plant often resulted from the largesse of traction owners and real estate boosters who counted on pseudo-Gothic quadrangles to lend prestige to neighboring subdivisions. The master of the Manhattan Elevated, Jay Gould, helped underwrite New York University's move to its Bronx "Heights" quarters, a site which lay astride the new steam railroad he was building into Westchester. In the 1890s, the horsecar promoters who boosted Westminster, seven miles outside Denver, aspired to make their Bible college another Northwestern, their straggling village another Evanston. Edgar G. Lewis, the erratic publisher, shrewdly concocted his "University City" between the Washington University campus and the St. Louis World's Fair grounds in Forest Park. If only his credit had lasted, Lewis could have prospered as the city grew into these western suburbs. As late as 1925, UCLA's benefactors hoped the school would anchor posh Bel Air and Westwood in western Los Angeles.

The business decisions which had the greatest impact on suburban development, however, were those which underwrote the trolley revolution. Soon after Frank J. Sprague mated electric power with the Union Passenger horsecars of Richmond, Virginia, in 1887, promoters found that electricity slashed operating costs and could move vehicles ten miles per hour in open country. By 1891, "electrics" captured 40 per cent of all traction mileage, while the imminent conversion of anachronistic cable roads and horsecars attracted the attention of large-scale financiers. The Consolidated Traction Company of New Jersey, behind which stood Prudential Insurance and United States Senator John F. Dryden, laced together the Oranges, Bloomfield, and Montclair across Essex County. Reflecting the vast resources of Thomas Fortune Ryan and William C. Whitney and their ties with Tammany boss Richard Croker, the Union Railway replaced the decrepit "bobtail" cars in the Bronx and Westchester and reached White Plains and Scarsdale with electrics by 1895. Henry M. Whitney's West End Street Railway brought high-class suburbs like Somerville, Brookline, and Cambridge within minutes of Boston's "Hub." By 1902, twenty-five giants out of 817 companies controlled more than one fifth of street railway mileage in the country. The largest operators also plunged ahead with high-speed electrics that ran on standard-gauge track. Detroit's "interurbans" provided downtown service to Palmer Park and Royal Oak. After twenty years of construction, Henry E. Huntington's Pacific Electric cars ran from the San Bernardino Valley in the east to Santa Monica's beaches, from San Fernando in the north to the oilfields at San Pedro—an empire that crisscrossed 1,164 miles around the old Los Angeles core.

Ironically, the electrics' phenomenal success brought on grave transit crises, as central business districts choked under new waves of suburban traffic. "Look at the city of Detroit," lamented a University of Michigan engineer in 1915. "You couldn't get any more [street] cars there. It is nothing but a moving platform now. If they expect to have more cars, they will have to build elevateds or subways." In city after city business leaders and politicians, anxious about trolley-clogged downtowns, struggled to separate suburban passenger service from local street traffic. In the 1890s, William Vanderbilt sunk the New York Central's tracks below Manhattan's street level, providing the Hudson, Harlem, and New Haven Divisions for the first time with transit routes without grade crossings down to Grand Central Station. The Pennsylvania Railroad spent $112 million tunneling under the Hudson and East Rivers, blasting under Manhattan's schist to give electric-train passengers, from New Jersey and Long Island, direct access to magnificent new Penn Station at Thirty-fourth Street. Viaduct or subway "loops" down Chicago's State Street, under Philadelphia's Market Street, and under Boston's State Street testified to the determination of downtown elites and their "Tammany" allies to maintain the vitality of the central district. The fear of commercial extinction was no less acute in Los Angeles, where lines of streetcars jammed the old *pueblo* core. But the city's political and business leaders failed in 1906, 1917, and 1926 at attempts for authority to con-

struct a downtown Pacific Electric underground or viaduct.
The city's weak Democratic machine, backed by the relatively
small immigrant population, vitiated by "progressivism" at
the turn of the century, could hardly ram through a downtown bond issue over the vetoes of the Americanized suburbs.

By the turn of the century, metropolitan expansion also
rested upon those downtown salesmen who packaged suburbia for varied classes in the city. From Manhattan offices, fu-
gitive southern and rural publicists like Walter Hines Page
and Liberty Hyde Bailey led the siren call "back to nature."
Their slickly edited, brightly illustrated *Suburban Life, Countryside, Outing,* and similar magazines shrewdly played on the
anxieties of the urban elite. Articles urged the removal of
stunted tenement children to "fresh air" camps or advised
how bucolic surroundings could restore a businessman's
frazzled nerves. Advertising quickly took on the new suburban idiom. Gibson girls with Palmolive-pure complexions
sunned on country club verandahs, while golfers eyed
Cadillacs parked in the driveways—such were the images that
tantalized the wealthy. Much suburban encomiums came
from trolley executives, most notably from Henry M. Whitney, promoter of Boston's giant West End Street Railway.
Whitney tirelessly harangued metropolitan audiences, churned
out editorials, and provided colorful copy for his view that
trolleys and suburban cottages would eradicate social unrest.
Other streetcar managers dressed up the outskirts in gaudy
colors for the masses. The Census Bureau reported in 1902
that one third of the nation's transit roads had built, owned,
or leased parks, lager gardens, and country resorts. While
some were dignified groves, like Cincinnati's Ludlow Lagoon,
operated in the Kentucky countryside by the Covington inter-
urban, others were honky-tonks, like Chicago's "Sans Souci,"
between Washington Park and Race Track, which offered a
Japanese pagoda, electric fountain, a Temple of Palmistry,
and shooting galleries. Thanks to the trolley corporations' ag-
gressive promotional campaigns, millions glimpsed suburbia
in "Coney Island style" fairgrounds or in more sedate, con-
templative retreats in the country.

THE STRUGGLE FOR THE CORRIDORS

Although trolleys, interurbans, and steam railroads distended the shape of the city, the nickel ride, in particular, foreshortened the social distance between classes which suburbanites had come to accept by the 1890s. Built-up areas of many cities, the census reported in 1902, "consist of long fingers or tentacles reaching out from the more solid centers, each owing its growth to a radiating street railway." Whether along Bloomfield Avenue connecting Newark with the Oranges, or Vincennes Avenue from Chicago's Loop down to Blue Island, or Commonwealth Avenue which brought Boston commuters back home to Brighton and Brookline, the electrics greatly increased contact between income levels hitherto separated by more inefficient and expensive transit. To the consternation of the wealthy "man with the checkbook," trolleys seemed to serve as a magnet for multiple dwellings, saloons, and the "man with the dinner pail."

Beginning in the 1890s, many suburbs underwent what sociologist Herbert Gans has called "definitional struggles" to determine whether working- or middle-class culture would prevail along transit corridors. The running battle which the Montclair Citizens Committee of 100 had fought since the mid-1880s to limit saloons along Bloomfield Avenue boiled over in 1894 when North Jersey Street Railway sought a franchise for its "electrics." The hilltoppers who could afford carriages to the Delaware and Lackawanna train station thought the trolley's moral incursions outweighed its boon to speculative real estate. "By so much as Montclair is brought nearer to Newark," a Protestant minister pointed out, "by so much is Newark brought nearer to Montclair, and the character of the town would be changed." Many antifranchisers also doubled as supporters of the "Cambridge Plan," after these Montclair residents learned how the Boston suburb had used its YMCA and "union" church meetings to evangelize against the saloon. In 1894, the upland Protestants voted changes in local town government to limit Irish-Democratic strength to just one ward straddling the thoroughfare. The new majority easily imposed high licenses on saloonkeepers and stymied for several years North Jersey's franchise efforts.

The traction lobby eventually won its fight, however, and the new century saw increased fears of newcomers and property deterioration. "Montclair is a town without a slum," boasted a 1907 account, admitting, "to be sure . . . poorer quarters along the railroad tracks, and off the business streets . . . [where] may be found the few, the very few saloons." This complacency ended with the opening of the McAdoo tubes under the Hudson River and census estimates of a startling influx of Italian and Negro residents. In 1908 the Montclair Civic Association held a planning conference and called in landscape architect John Nolen to suggest improvements. Nolen urged beautification of the Lackawanna railway station, development of a town hall-civic center-school complex, regulated cornice heights and Georgian brick or Tudor half-timber for commercial structures along Bloomfield Avenue. Taxpayers balked at such costly social cohesion and eventually chose cheaper, simpler restrictions. By the First World War, the suburb had adopted prohibition by local option, centralized planning, and established a commission government to contain the spread of downtown "blight."

The Montclair experience typified confrontations along many corridors opened up by the nickel trolley. Struggles usually were waged by local "town improvement" clubs, formed in the 1880s to "cultivate public spirit and foster town pride, quicken intellectual life, promote good fellowship, and uplift the sagging New England village." Now this civic gospel focused on breaches in the metropolitan line, whether Flushing's Good Citizenship League which in 1894 rallied against a trolley and a Manhattan-run race track or the Scarsdale "Town Club" founded in 1904 to watch encroachments by both New York City and White Plains. "Let the suburbs shame the city," urged the American Civic Association, "with clean and sightly homes on model streets, with public utilities held subject to public use and public beauty, and the city will profit." The trolley zone's ugliness particularly offended suburban civic pride. The billboard which "follows the railroads, trolley lines, and boulevards out into the suburbs," met organized opponents in East Walpole, Milton, and Wellesley. These societies in metropolitan Boston launched the Massachusetts Civic League to co-ordinate the attack against the "tramp menace" and the multiple dwelling and endorsed the "Direct or Crowbar Approach" against outdoor advertising. Improvers in Brookline, disturbed by trolley unsightliness, transformed Beacon Street from a fifty-foot roadway into a "splendid parkway" with a central streetcar "reservation" screened by shrubbery. Other groups emerged as protectors of shade trees "menaced by corridor gas mains, utility poles, and wires." The East Orange Shade Tree Commission borrowed the New Jersey Republicans' "New Idea" rhetoric to attack power companies who "ruthlessly mutilated and destroyed trees along highways for the passage of overhead wires." Transit corridors also harbored "dust evils," tuberculosis, and other insidious germs from the horse droppings scattered by speeding vehicles. Dust-suppression campaigns went on with particular vigor in Brookline and Arlington, Massachusetts; Tuxedo Park, Garden City, and Mount Vernon, New York, and other high-class areas. Pasadena typified many communities when it went to extra expense to make Marengo Avenue a beautiful "oiled road."

Faced also with the spread of downtown saloons, suburbs launched local-option and high-license campaigns to contain Demon Rum. In Westchester County, communities which straddled busy travel routes took the earliest action. Scarsdale went "dry" in 1899, soon after trolley service improved on the White Plains Road; White Plains followed in 1905. Temperance reformers were well aware that votes to close down localities often depended upon the existence of convenient nearby saloon strips, "safety valves" for the suburbanite to drink or buy packaged spirits. By 1900, Cambridge, the largest liquor-free suburb in the country, was followed by dry Somerville, Chelsea, Malden, Newton, Everett, Medford, Melrose, Brookline, and Reading. The Massachusetts Total Abstinence Society acknowledged, however, that these contained residents who "could get all the liquor they required" in the Hub, but who "preferred to keep the saloon away from their homes." This attitude was apparent in an 1899 referendum, when teetotal Cambridge voted against state-wide prohibition, no doubt, to keep packaged liquor available in neighboring communities. By 1916, from Winnetka to Oak Park and Riverside to Berwyn, a broad saloonless belt had formed around Chicago. Here, too, drinks could be bought in Blue Island, Cicero, and other nearby working-class sections. In 1913 communities like Hawthorne, Lyndhurst, and Ridgefield Park had taken up provisions in New Jersey's Walsh Act to institute a local prohibition option as well as commission government. When the legislature enacted state-wide local option in 1917, the suburbs that took the pledge included most of those west of Newark: East and South Orange, Montclair, Rutherford, North and South Caldwell. In the meantime, many Garden State towns made do with selective enforcement, like Englewood, which initiated a "dry Sunday" campaign in 1906 and clamped down on saloons along Palisades Avenue, but allowed the Town and Golf clubs to operate on Bergen County licenses.

Suburbs, served by commuter railroads and farther away from the trolley's incursions, could resort to less urgent devices to maintain a homogeneous environment. Ornamental arches were the rage in Southern California, where realtors felt they lent entire tracts "that air of exclusiveness and privacy which characterizes the private villa." Other planners urged beautification of train stations and commuter plazas. The Boston and Albany's efforts to clothe its terminals with tailored shrubbery won the laurel "Garden Railroad" from appreciative commuters. After the founding of Brookline's Clyde Park Country Club in the mid-1880s and the golf craze at the turn of the century, the private sports club often served as the nucleus around which local government developed. With property owners empowered to vote and make policy, the "incorporated club" controlled garbage pickups, police patrols, road repair, and street lighting from the Heathcote Colony in Scarsdale to the "Homes Association" of Palos

Verdes on the Pacific. *American City,* an ardent champion of "progressivism," found the "Civic League" of Roland Park, Maryland, to be the exemplary commission government, where trustees who managed the interests of property owners literally applied the ideal of "business principles" to politics.

Areas faced with direct urban encroachment, however, required more systematic controls. "Slum germs are at work," warned the Massachusetts Civic League in 1911. "Foreigners are coming in increasing numbers, and with them are also coming the shack, the converted house . . . the familiar frame tenement, and the wooden 'three decker'." The last, a League spokesman claimed, had spread throughout eastern New England "like the cholera or yellow fever." Winthrop, a short trolley ride east of the Hub, had enough triple deckers to give it an undesired "Dorchestry" look. The Brookline planning board complained that "stores of unattractive type" had encroached upon property lines and spoiled Beacon Street's "generous, dignified appearance." Struggling against the multiple dwelling, the Civic League lobbied a tenement-house bill for small towns through the State Legislature in 1912. The law which went into effect by local town referendum, limited building height, bulk, yard space, and prohibited certain wooden-frame tenements. Armed with their trusty stereopticons and exhibit booths, Bay Staters barraged their communities with housing publicity. Within three years, twenty-three towns had implemented the act, nearly all in the suburban belts around Boston, Quincy, and Lynn.

Philadelphia's Main Line suburbs, finding themselves in the "danger zone" of the city's westward expansion, counterattacked in 1911 with sophisticated social surveys conducted by professional charity workers. They uncovered delapidated rowhouses, rear tenements, and backed-up privies along the Lancaster Turnpike in Haverford; jerry-built hovels near the Rosemont trolley; and "squalid" multiple dwellings on Highland Avenue in Wayne. An alarmed coalition which called itself the Main Line Housing Association pressed suburban health boards for strict local inspections. Civic leaders denied, however, that this effort to upgrade housing would price apartment rentals on the Main Line much beyond what the working class could afford.

THE EMERGENCE OF SUBURBAN REGIONALISM

Gradually, after the turn of the century, isolated community struggles to contain the corridors developed into a regional suburban consciousness. In part, this wider viewpoint resulted from encroachments by the trolley-borne city. Stimulus came from suburban magazines, "progressive" planning ideas, and the city beautiful movement, which had flourished after the 1893 Chicago World's Fair. Individual communities had also gotten together to settle specific problems as well as relationships with downtown. By World War I a co-ordinated response had evolved to oppose metropolitan expansion.

Suburbs first began serious mutual discussions within the framework of "special improvements districts" which had sprung up to handle the growing burden of sewage disposal, water supply, and road repair. These were not mere patronage districts erected by the GOP during the Civil War, but service bureaucracies, paid for by suburban tax levies, and using electricity, telephones, cheap asphalt, and other new inventions that signaled suburban independence from downtown technology. Many traction experts, utilities engineers, and corporate lawyers had now moved out from the city, bringing their regional viewpoints and political connections to suburb-wide coalitions. In 1898, a pollution crisis in New Jersey's Passaic River Valley coincided with downtown boasts about a "greater Newark" absorbing her hapless suburbs in the valley. The Oranges, Irvington, and Vailsburg sent plenopotentiaries to parley with Newark about extending her sewer lines throughout the region. Protracted negotiations, however, did not result in annexation to Newark but rather in the legislature's creation of the Passaic Valley Sewer District, supported with assessments from enrolled communities, which provided access to a large outfall sewer in Newark Bay. Annexations beyond the Boston peninsula in the 1860s and

1870s were now replaced by successive layers of special districts: Metropolitan Sewage District, formed in 1889; Parks, 1893; Water, 1895; Water and Sewerage, 1901; combined Metropolitan, 1919; Planning, 1923; Transit, 1929. Each "authority" had its own tax base and bureaucratic superstructure. Through them the suburbs gained the technology and political leverage that offered an alternative to annexation.

Suburban opinion inevitably drifted from talk of districts to anticipated regional growth. Westchester County planning originated in anxieties about the deteriorated spine of settlement along the Bronx River north of the New York City line. "Where the riverbed was wide enough to justify a settlement," an expert recalled, "population came and of a class which could not improve, and must perforce, defile the surroundings." In 1907, Scarsdale Republicans convinced the State Legislature to create a special corridor in Westchester and Bronx Counties under the aegis of a Bronx River Parkway Commission. But while this body labored against "centers of disorder and disease," deterioration had extended far beyond its jurisdiction. Between 1900 and 1910, Westchester grew at an unprecedented rate. New York Central and New Haven steam depots had become crowded with "ramshackle" buildings, lumberyards, light industry, and multiple dwellings. Urged by realtors and the Chamber of Commerce, County Supervisors in 1914 appointed a Planning Commission to advise on "the best land to be selected for residence districts, with the class of residents which naturally, because of topographical and commercial surroundings, would occupy such land." Mandated to inventory overall county needs, planners actually focused on worrisome eyesores: a "Coney Island" trolley park razed at Rye Beach, overhead streetcar wires screened at White Plains' Broadway Park, and civic plazas in place of congested flathouses along the corridors in New Rochelle and White Plains.

A similar understanding of planning emerged from conferences, starting in 1913, between metropolitan Boston and vocal suburban representatives on Massachusetts planning boards and the State Homestead Commission. Downtown spokesmen, including Mayor James Michael Curley, dwelled on the tenement-house congestion, city fire and police efficiency, and plans to upgrade health care. In contrast, suburban delegates, distressed by a "general lack of harmony" in their localities, saw planning as largely an aesthetic venture in

towns [that] are more or less nondescript character, with narrow streets and congested traffic; elaborate buildings surrounded by cheap, tumbledown structures, and with no approaches in keeping with the character of the buildings; fine residential districts with cheap and unsanitary tenement properties adjoining them.

Here the litmus test was suburban reaction to the Homestead Commission's proposals to take the pressure off crowded Boston by relocating working-class homes on the metropolitan outskirts. To the suburban-dominated planning boards, city deconcentration meant the location of "model tenements," not in low-density suburbs, but in the immigrant wards of peripheral cities like Lynn.

Suburbs in Delaware and Montgomery counties, finding themselves in the "danger zone" of South Philadelphia's westward expansion, appropriated regional planning as a sophisticated defense. While the Main Line Housing Association stoically acknowledged that "Wherever communities are built, the poor, the day laborer, and the mechanic are needed," its members strenuously policed substandard housing largely inhabited by Negroes, Italians, and other "foreigners." Campaigning for restrictive sanitary inspections, importing downtown social workers, and seeking the Massachusetts precedent of a tenement law for small towns, the Association exhausted the usual "progressive" techniques for housing uplift. Looking for greater political leverage, Main Line leaders in 1912 sponsored a series of conferences of all local improvement groups within a twenty-five-mile radius of Philadelphia's City Hall. At one session John Nolen, Frederic C. Howe, and experts from New York's Bureau of Municipal Research described the latest advances in the civic revival. At the Ardmore YMCA delegates heard Philadelphia's chief of public works herald Mayor Rudolph Blankenburg's "great reconstruction work" which welcomed the "participation" of the outlying communities. But the suburban leaders had already begun to think beyond downtown initiatives. Some urged suburbs pool resources to overcome the "absence of radial and circumferencial thoroughfares" which prevented intersuburban contact, while an Ardmore representative argued that with community co-operation, "a united front could be presented before the legislature." In November, 1912, enthusiasts launched a Suburban Co-Operative Planning Association, which organized housing lectures and exhibits, sponsored contests for the design of "model tenements," and cajoled more "progressive" builders to improve working-class dwellings. When the Association sought official sanction from the Pennsylvania legislature in 1913, they strenuously lobbied for absolute local control over all development decisions. The legislature obliged with a Metropolitan Planning District, a harmless advisory board on which twelve suburban delegates could readily veto proposals made by three from Philadelphia. Whether in Westchester County, greater Boston, or metropolitan Philadelphia, suburbanites fluently spoke the argot of progressive regionalism, but never relinquished a localism that remained staunchly aloof from downtown.

SEMIDETACHED AMBIENCE; SUBURBS FOR THE MASSES IN THE TWENTIES

During the 1920s, the spectacular growth of upper-income suburbs borne by the auto obscured those fundamental trends that continued methodically to expand the metropolitan hinterland. During the decade, Glendale, California, grew by 3,000 per cent, Beverly Hills by nearly 2,500 per cent; and Shaker Heights, Ohio by 1,000 per cent. Car registrations spiraled upward, prompting social theorists to envision new unbounded communities, "radial frontiers" pioneered by motorists. Census figures soberly confirmed what sociologist Harlan Paul Douglass called the "suburban trend." In 1920, the Bureau counted over 11,000,000 people living beyond city boundaries in sixty-two metropolitan areas. By 1930, population of the outer rings had expanded at twice the rate of their core cities and contained more than 17,000,000—perhaps one in every seven Americans. Still, much of this growth represented the intensification of earlier patterns: the decentralization of industry, the movement of retail stores beyond the central business district, and the modernization of commuter transit. Although the auto's impact was undeniable, it proved hardly decisive in those large cities with established transit networks. Millions rode crowded "Els," subways, and streetcars (supplemented by bus service) out to garden apartments, duplex bungalows, or semidetached houses. For just $600 down and $48 per month, second-generation Americans emerging from inner-city tenements could share a patch of grass and some sunlight in the city limits.

Thousands of manufacturers, encouraged by outlying belt-line railroads, long-distance electric transmission, and telephone exchanges, sought industrial space on the metropolitan periphery. The 1910 census found that in the previous decade an increase in the number of suburban factory jobs far outpaced the central cities'. Once Boston's "streetcar suburb," Cambridge now had one fifth of Boston's industrial output and was soon to become the fourth largest industrial city in New England. Paterson's famed silk and worsted mills, along with their "operatives," had spilled into Garfield and the "Botany" section of Clifton. Metalworks, printing lofts, and food processors had drifted from Manhattan into the deepened tidal streams of Greater New York. The shift came most dramatically where heavy industry required sprawling acreage. As early as the 1890s, Chicago realtors had packaged special "industrial districts," with railroad sidings and utility conduits, far from the Loop. The most famous was Calumet Harbor, recovered from lake dunes, and lined by 1910 with vast steelworks and chemical plants. Industrial satellites ringed Chicago on the south and west: Cicero (the home of Western Electric's giant Hawthorne plant), Harvey, Blue Island, Chicago Heights, Hammond, Indiana, and the huge U. S. Steelworks in Gary. Henry Ford's "on line" assembly factories changed the social landscape of greater Detroit. He located thousands of jobs beyond the city line—at Highland Park, Northville, Flat Rock, and, of course, River Rouge.

By the 1920s, not only did more urbanites work on the metropolitan periphery, but more shopped and enjoyed their entertainment there as well. New commercial subcenters sprouted at transit intersections, where homebound commuters switched from trains to streetcars. National chains gravitated to these high-volume locations; United Cigar Stores, Walgreen's, and Woolworth's attracted customers who preferred "neighborhood" convenience. As early as 1910, Chicago had six distinct subcenters, including Sixty-third and Halsted on the southwest side, the second largest shopping district outside the Loop; and 111th and South Michigan Avenue, which served Pullman and Blue Island. Life in New York's "outer boroughs" pulsed around the 149th Street "Hub" in the Bronx and "downtown" Flushing and Jamaica in Queens. The streetcar concentration at the Market Street "El" and 69th Street made Upper Darby the major shopping center for both West Philadelphia and nearby suburbs. After dark, these areas glittered with neon-trimmed movie "palaces" built by theater chains that met the outlying audiences' demand for the latest "Broadway" movies. By 1924 Balaban and Katz and lesser-known chains had constructed theaters in all of Chicago's subcenters and had bought out vaudeville theaters in Aurora, Elgin, Des Plaines, and other communities. That same year, Loew's entered the suburban New York market, taking over a "first run" house in White Plains. Department stores, which had extended telephone order and delivery service, grudgingly began to trek after their affluent customers. Upstart competitors generally led the exodus, like Wieboldt's, which in 1910 became the first Chicago department store to branch beyond the Loop. Sears, Roebuck, wary of downtown competition and closely attuned to motorists' buying habits, began a concerted subcenter strategy for its housewares and auto-supply stores in 1926. By contrast, Marshall Field's waited until 1929 to open specialty branches in upper-income Evanston, Oak Park, and Lake Forest.

While the motorist monopolized newspaper space and advertising copy, the straphanger, whether in a railroad train, streetcar or motor coach, carried the burden of suburban commuting. The auto made considerable strides in smaller metropolises like Kansas City, Missouri, where 41 per cent drove into the business district in the mid-twenties; or Washington, D.C., with 55 per cent. But in Boston only one in four drove; Chicago one in five; and Detroit, the "Motor City," counted just 18 per cent in 1927. The spectacular growth of Long Island and Westchester County depended less upon the automobile than upon the enormous expansion of the Long Island and New York Central rail service. Suburban Nassau County's population nearly quadrupled between 1910 and 1930, but the Long Island's commuter haul, thanks to its huge Sunnyside yards (completed in 1910) and overhead electrification that went into effect in 1924, expanded ten times. Roads linking suburbs to central cities, long under the thumb of county politics and debt ceilings, looked archaic, in contrast.

Highway engineers less responsible to suburban commuters than truck farmers took a dim view toward "speedways" for the wealthy that would, as a Wayne County, Michigan, engineer remarked in 1915, "array one class against another." Well into the twenties, traffic experts, co-ordinated by the nation's chief engineer, Secretary of Commerce Herbert Hoover, reflected this conservatism. Instead of new roads, the professionals urged widened lanes, grade separations, bans on "promiscuous access and parking," and traffic lights synchronized to "platoon" cars as acceptable expedients. An alternative had existed, of course, in the aesthetic drives that for decades had graced metropolitan park systems. In the wake of the city beautiful movement, landscape architects urged that these "limited access" parkways should "skirt" around outlying town centers rather than funnel bumper-to-bumper cars on main streets. Not until the Bronx Park commissioners built the Bronx River Parkway (opened in 1925) and public works czar Robert Moses let the dirt fly on the Long Island highway system in the 1930s, did motorists benefit from high-speed traffic arteries that bypassed commercial intersections.

For millions of urban dwellers the better life amounted to an affordable, compromised suburbia within walking distance or motor-coach fare of the "Els" in the "outer wards." Suburban Westchester and Nassau counties soared spectacularly during the twenties, adding 350,000 residents, yet this was less than half those who found semisuburban neighborhoods *within* New York City, like Flushing and Jamaica, Queens; Pelham Bay in the Bronx; and Midwood or Flatbush in Brooklyn. This nether world between old tenement ghettos and isolated suburban freeholds existed around garden apartments, rowhouses, or semidetached duplexes (mortgaged to a building and loan association) on a "block" whose tone, at least, was determined by the settlement of "coreligionists." For middle-class Jews in South Philadelphia, upward mobility meant moving west to "Strawberry Mansion" and joining B'nai Jeshurun Synagogue. Later in the twenties, this migration extended beyond Fairmount Park to Wynnfield, with the aid of Jewish builders who subcontracted carpentry, masonry, and brickwork within the ethnic community. Eastern Queens and South Brooklyn were patchworks of Irish, Germans, Jews, and Italians lured by the mass transit lines from Manhattan and downtown Brooklyn. Large-scale developers like Bryan L. Kennelly in Woodhaven, E. O. Jahrsdorfer in Ridgewood, and Lewis H. May, Andrew N. Miller, and the Morgenthau organization in Jackson Heights and Richmond Hill reached the Irish, German, and Jewish communities through ethnic media such as the *Yiddisher Morgen Journal* which boasted that its real estate ads reached "the investing class of Jews." On a finer scale, relying on a Catholic church or synagogue as ethnic compass points, Italian contractors erected rows of one-family stuccoes on East Thirty-seventh Street, Flatbush; Irish developers projected two-family brick houses in Ridgewood; Jewish realtors handled the subdivision of Edgemere.

These ethnic concentrations in the outer wards met suburbia largely on their own terms. Many could not have moved without the two-family houses, bought with a down payment borrowed from parents or in-laws, which perpetuated (through the upstairs apartment) close family relations that had existed in the tenements. Families and friends settled in tandem, honeycombing the streets with relationships dominated by family ties rather than "neighborliness." For the well-off middle class, Wednesday afternoon Mah-Jongg or Friday night pinochle brought city acquaintances together. But for most in the lower-middle and working class, leisure meant six o'clock suppers, radios on in the "living room," or "stoop" lounging until mosquitoes forced them indoors. Despite the 25′ x 100′ lots, families cultivated a new privacy, broken down only by their children, who played basketball or stickball in the driveways and loitered under streetlights or outside corner candy stores. Catholic churches and Jewish synagogues held greater importance in defining the neighborhood's ethnic identity than in providing a fulcrum for associational activities. They became secular "centers" for the community's intense worship of organized recreation, for its homeowners' association, and political life. Generally, however, those families that had predominated religious life in the old neighborhoods simply continued in the new, leading the men's clubs, sodalities, and sisterhoods. For middle-class breadwinners, haggard from a trip on the subway, the six-room boxes offered a new privacy, which they jealously guarded.

STANDARDS AND STANDARDIZATION

By the middle 1920s, realtors had reached a consensus on how to settle the new suburbanite in regions outside city limits. "The good subdivider," "a creator, a man of vision and achievement," worked best on a generous scale, preferably three hundred acres or more, on a site where natural or man-made boundaries limited an otherwise "endless spread of urban expansion." He preferred 40′ x 100′ lots, reserving side alleys for underground utility conduits and auto "strips." Unsightly overhead utility lines and back alleys had become "a thing of the past." Proper deed restrictions assured home buyers about "the cost of buildings, build-back, race, etc."

Developers emphasized careful deed exclusions, where practical, against Negroes and other minorities who might drag down values. Experts, like the improvers of Shaker Heights, Ohio, advised a careful separation between modes of transit access: "It is a mistake to put high-grade, refined residents on a car line which is used largely by a foreign population or a low class of laborers." Others relied on the golf craze to sell home lots. "The American businessman wants his golf," insisted Hugh E. Prather, who successfully incorporated the game into his Highland Park subdivision outside of Dallas. One landscaper alone, Tom Bendelow, laid out seven hundred courses throughout the nation and Canada during the decade.

Many of the newest developments, whether aimed at a working- or high-class market, employed several or all of these design techniques. The Van Sweringen brothers, who moved from Cleveland traction to real estate, controlled trolley approaches as well as the overall design of their Shaker Square. While architects fashioned a traction depot and commercial center into a pseudonineteenth-century village, elaborate deed restrictions prohibited multiple dwellings, saloons, and discordant home designs. At Los Angeles' Palos Verdes Estates, whose rambling hillsides offered spectacular views of the Pacific, the Olmsted Brothers' surveyors followed natural contours, laying a central streetcar thoroughfare and subsidiary motor drives. Lots varied from 60' x 125' to an acre, but all home designs had to meet specifications of a paid "art jury." Six business centers provided community focal points, around which grouped a limited number of multiple dwellings and less expensive bungalow courts, which the Olmsteds screened from lower-density acreage through the use of school parks and golf courses. Even Torrance, another Los Angeles project designed to attract workers in the San Pedro industrial district, reflected aesthetic rudiments. Here again, the Olmsteds designed a broad avenue separating residential districts from a special industrial preserve. While forbidding tenements and boardinghouses as well as saloons, the land company sold frame and concrete bungalows "on easy terms" to "mechanics." For more recent arrivals, it reserved "a special section . . . as a foreign quarter, unlike in every respect the usual Ghetto and Latin quarter."

Suburban retailing proved even more difficult to contain with the onset of the automobile. Small business extensions alongside trolley routes looked tidy when compared to the rank commercial growth stimulated by this new mobility. The car encouraged roadside stands, "gasoline fill-ups," and stores, creating miles of ugly "string streets" which distressed aesthetes, "quality" realtors, and downtown merchants alike. A few subdividers experimented with regulated business arcades and commercial blocks integrated into their design. Both Roland Park, outside Baltimore, and the Van Sweringens' Shaker Heights clustered retail stores otherwise prohibited from residential streets. But merchandisers, convinced that sales meant window displays close to the stream of traffic, even if double or triple parked, remained conservative. In the early twenties, however, developers showed how retailers could break away from the linear street arrangement to one which profitably met the demands of the outlying motorist. J. C. Nichols' Country Club Plaza in Kansas City, Missouri, and Hugh Prather's River Oaks Shopping Center both employed unified "business" architecture, landscaping, and off-street parking. Later, in 1931, at Highland Park outside Dallas, Prather turned his stores away from the main thoroughfare and surrounded them with customers' parking lots. The wisdom of locating retail trade where suburbanites already lived particularly made sense to new retail chains, anxious to avoid direct competition with the established department stores in the central business district. By the late 1920s, Sears, Roebuck, followed by Montgomery Ward, carefully picked sites at the confluence of highways. Large, reinforced-concrete, windowless structures, surrounded by a hundred parking slots and dominated by the bold Sears logo, became a familiar sight on outlying crossroads. Led by Nichols, who was emphatic that "neighborhood" groceries, meat markets, and drugstores need be clustered at no less than half-mile intervals, landscape architects casually integrated the park-and-shop arrangement in planned subdivisions. Located on the "home-going side" of an arterial boulevard, on the tract's periphery, the shopping center became an anchorage for low-income housing and multiple dwellings as well as a focal point for large acreages of detached homes.

To preserve these inchoate patterns amidst the motorcar's anarchy, suburban developers resorted to zoning. In 1916 Manhattanites had used zoning to prevent the spillover of immigrant garment loft "operatives" into fashionable Fifth Avenue and imposed a "comprehensive" zoning ordinance, the nation's first, on all of New York City. The device epitomized much of the "scientific" rationalism and "business efficiency" of progressive reform. Adherents explained that every metropolis contained areas "naturally" meant for exclusive industrial, commercial, or residential functions. Once these "zones" were identified, overall restrictions on building height, bulk, and use would protect and enhance their "natural" development. The idea's chief apostle, Flatbush lawyer Edward M. Bassett, advised local enthusiasts across the country, compiled digests of legal decisions, and publicized model zoning codes. He resolved to protect the wholesome, "old-fashioned village center" against the onslaught of the auto-borne metropolis and its "garages and filling stations," and championed the single, detached home on a generous garden plot against its mortal enemy, "the out-of-place apartment house." His convictions had legions of supporters. "A single-house region," observed George C. Whipple, in a typical pamphlet, *Zoning and Health,* sponsored by the Massachusetts Federation of Planning Boards, "once infected with an apartment house tends to accumulate other apartments, and the neighborhood tends to change from a stable, home-owning population to a shifting, renting class, a class lacking in neighborliness and civic pride and leading an impoverished family life." If they belonged anywhere in the suburbs, apartment houses had to be relegated to major traffic arteries or next to industrial plants to enable factory workers to walk to their jobs. Zoning in many new suburbs gave legal sanction to realtors already inclined to prohibit prewar places of idle amusement from residential streets. Away went barbershops, luncheonettes, candy stores, garages, poolrooms, and cheap movie houses—banished to thoroughfares zoned "commercial" on the edges of subdivisions. Here, as well, Bassett argued against casual business clutter. A "freeway" he defined as a "strip of land dedicated to *movement* over which the abutting owner has no right of light, air, or access," a concept vital to the emerging view of the "bypass highway."

Prohibition campaigns, housing reforms, and planning, all were absorbed by the new interest in zoning, the most ingenious guarantor of the new segregated life-style. Only thirty-five American municipalities adopted comprehensive zoning ordinances up to 1920, while 438 joined the trend in the next five years. Scarsdale enacted New York State's first suburban law in 1922. Three years later, when builders applied to the Town Zoning Board for a "variance" to erect multiple dwellings with stores near the railroad station, the Scarsdale Board, with Bassett's help, denied the move and successfully fought the encroachment in the courts. New Jersey communities such as Englewood, Hackensack, and Montclair used zoning to keep large Negro populations in well-defined multiple-dwelling reserves. In Nutley, a suburban village up the Passaic between Paterson and Newark, an ordinance contested a Greek immigrant's opening of a fruit stand in a "residential" section. While the Nutley code stumbled in the State Supreme Court, the New Jersey League of Municipalities carried on the struggle and put a state-wide enabling ordinance on the ballot, a referendum which the voters approved in 1927. By the late twenties, cities, already well girdled by low-density communities, were ringed as well by suburban zoning laws and new *ad hoc* suburban interest groups. Organizations surrounding New York City included: the Fairfield County Planning Association, the Westchester County Planning Federation, the Passaic Planning Association, the Essex County Zoning Conference, and the Bergen County League of Municipalities. They eschewed any earlier sentimentalism about regional interdependence and working-class "model tenements" in favor of hard-nosed lobbying and legal fights to uphold the zoning settlement.

The Commerce Department's Division of Building and Housing, joining forces with local groups, emerged as the chief co-ordinator of the movement toward subdivision control. The Division distributed proven house designs and model structural specifications to modernize builders' practices. With Secretary Herbert Hoover's enthusiastic approval, it supported "Better Homes for America," a nationwide federation of five thousand neighborhood improvement clubs aimed at upgrading the suburban environment and encouraging the building of "sound, beautiful, single-family houses." Zoners recognized the Division as their "official headquarters," from which flowed a raft of model ordinances and pamphlets, as well as Bassett's legal digests. Its surveys of local zoning and planning codes accurately charted their national spread. The fitting climax to these efforts to control and plan for the new automobile communities was President Hoover's Conference on Home Building and Home Ownership in 1931. By then, however, the Wall Street collapse had frozen further residential construction. Metropolitan Cleveland found itself with 375,000 lots, 45 per cent of them empty. Overzealous real estate activity had given Detroit 1,250,000 lots, enough for the population of three Motor Cities. Within several spring seasons, depression weeds had grown tall enough to cover stakes pounded in with such hope months before.

The outward rush after World War II has largely obscured the slow incremental process which suburbanized a seventh of the population during the century before 1930. To some the whole process seemed a formless chaos; a "wilderness of suburbs" was Lewis Mumford's plaintive critique in 1921. For all the apparent formlessness, the chaotic free market in housing, the individualism which dictated home buyers' decisions, the suburbs have long shown a surprising degree of communal control and forethought. By the late twenties, at the crest of this first great advance, suburban America had laid down the infrastructure to handle much future growth. Communities had added tangibles like water and sanitary districts, protean shopping centers, and a start at peripheral highways. They had joined to a precocious development of suburban vested interest, a deft use of zoning laws and regional planning conferences. In 1928, one of their own even made it to the White House. Herbert Hoover, staunch champion of the suburban way of life, defeated Al Smith, the Irish-Catholic hope from the expanding metropolis.

BIBLIOGRAPHY

SUBURBAN HISTORIOGRAPHY owes a great debt to the sociologists, particularly Harlan Paul Douglass' *The Suburban Trend* (New York, 1925), which recognized early the heterogeneous nature of suburban communities. The impact of social class behavior is explored in Herbert J. Gans, "Urbanism and Suburbanism as a Way of Life: A Re-evaluation of Definitions," in Arnold Rose, ed., *Human Behavior and Social Processes* (Boston, 1962) and his definitive *The Levittowners: Ways of Life and Politics in a New Suburban Community* (New York, 1967). The crucial "sector" theory of metropolitan expansion is delineated in Homer Hoyt's *The Structure and Growth of Residential Neighborhoods in American Cities* (Washington, 1939). Historians have just recently laid the groundwork for their own suburban analysis. Sam Bass Warner, Jr., *Streetcar Suburbs: The Process of Growth in Boston, 1870–1900* (Cambridge, 1969) brings a startling order to the laissez-faire "wilderness" of expanding Boston. Kenneth T. Jackson has written a perceptive pioneering survey, "The Crabgrass Frontier: 150 Years of Suburban Growth in America," in Raymond A. Mohl and James F. Richardson, eds., *The Urban Experience: Themes in American History* (Belmont, California, 1973). There are some excellent regional histories, including Robert M. Fogelson's institutional study, *The Fragmented Metropolis, Los Angeles, 1850–1930* (Cambridge, 1967); and Richard C. Wade and Harold M. Mayer's indispensable *Chicago* (Chicago, 1969).

No shortage exists, however, of histories of the naïve genre, some bittersweet reflections on the passing years and local "worthies," some multitomed "county" histories written for subscription, which poured from the Lewis Historical Publishing Company and similar presses before the First World War. Among the more interesting of the former are: Thomas C. Simonds, *History of South Boston, formerly Dorchester Neck, now Ward XII of the City of Boston* (Boston, 1857); Sidney D. Maxwell, *The Suburbs of Cincinnati, Sketches Historical and Descriptive* (Cincinnati, 1870); S. C. G. Watkins, *Reminiscences of Montclair* (New York, 1929); and Harry Hansen's serene view of one of the most posh communities, *Scarsdale* (New York, 1954). *The Autobiography of Edward M. Bassett* (New York, 1939) gives a mellow glimpse of suburban Brooklyn by the pioneer zoner. To these should be added a growing list of doctoral studies: Arthur E. LeGacy, "Improvers and Preservers: A History of Oak Park, Illinois, 1833–1940" (unpublished Ph.D. dissertation, University of Chicago, 1968); Harry A. A. Jebsen, "Blue Island, Illinois; The History of a Working-Class Suburb" (University of Cincinnati, 1971); and Joel Schwartz, "Community Building on the Bronx Frontier; Morrisania, 1848–1875" (University of Chicago, 1972). The evolving suburban scene can also be glimpsed in the pages of contemporary professional and special-interest magazines: *Country-Side Magazine and Suburban Life, Country Life in America, Landscape Architecture, American City,* and two that closely monitored the switch in transportation developments, *Street Railway Journal* and *Public Roads.*

On changing transit forms, see Glen E. Holt's wry survey, "The Changing Perception of Urban Pathology: An Essay on the Development of Mass Transit in the United States" in Kenneth T. Jackson and Stanley K. Schultz, eds., *Cities in American History* (New York, 1972); George Rogers Taylor's analysis of antebellum innovations, "The Beginnings of Mass Transportation in Urban America," *Smithsonian Journal of History,* I (1966). U. S. Bureau of the Census, *Special Reports on Street and Electric Railways* (Washington, 1902) provides a wealth of statistics and commentary on the streetcar revolution. The forces behind highway development in the twentieth century are outlined in American Asso-

ciation of State Highway Officials, *A Story of the Beginning,
Purposes, Growth, Activities and Achievements of the
AASHO* (Washington, 1964). The highway builders' matur-
ing philosophy is well discussed in W. Brewster Snow, ed., *The
Highway and the Landscape* (New Brunswick, 1959).

Several books survey varied motives which pushed the ur-
ban-industrial order into the countryside at the end of the
nineteenth century. Graham R. Taylor's *Satellite Cities: A
Study of Industrial Suburbs* (New York, 1915) is a balanced account of synthetic factory towns, while Stanley
Buder has detailed a remorseless paternalism in *Pullman: an
Experiment in Industrial Order and Community Planning,
1880–1930* (New York, 1967). Peter Schmitt, *Back to
Nature: The Arcadian Myth in Urban America* (New
York, 1969) illuminates the intense media campaign to
market "the country" for city appetites.

For material on metropolitan government and the annexa-
tion movement, see Kenneth T. Jackson's discussion which
strikes the right balance between the motives of planners and
politicians, "Metropolitan Government Versus Political Autonomy: Politics on the Crabgrass Frontier," in Jackson and
Schultz, *Cities in American History*. For Boston, see James
A. Merino, "A Great City and Its Suburbs: Attempts to
Integrate Metropolitan Boston, 1865–1920" (unpublished
Ph.D. dissertation, University of Texas, 1968); for Northern
New Jersey: Stuart Galishoff, "The Passaic Valley Trunk
Sewer," *New Jersey History*, LXXXVIII (Winter, 1970); and
for Los Angeles: Winston W. Crouch and Beatrice Diner-
man, *Southern California Metropolis* (Berkeley, 1963),
which all stress more the rationalism than the political impli-
cations of metropolitan structures. One should not overlook
two pioneering surveys of metropolitonism in the twenties:
Paul Studenski, *The Government of Metropolitan Areas in
the United States* (New York, 1930), and R. D. McKenzie,
"The Rise of Metropolitan Communities" in *Recent Social
Trends; Report of the President's Research Committee on Social Trends* (New York, 1933).

The suburbanization of the twenties is best seen in the

McKenzie article, Douglass' *Suburban Trend,* and the handy statistical compendium, U. S. Bureau of the Census, *Fifteenth Census, Growth of Metropolitan Areas* (Washington, 932). "Progressive" building and subdividing practices are described in the National Association of Real Estate Boards, *Home Building & Subdividing,* III (Chicago, 1925); President's Conference on Home Building and Home Ownership, *Reports* (Washington, 1931); and Better Homes in America, *Guidebook for Better Homes Campaign* (Washington, 1929). The spread of Los Angeles before and after the automobile age is well documented in Fogelson's *Fragmented Metropolis.* The automobile's impact on retailing is ominously surveyed in U. S. Department of Commerce, *Vehicular Traffic Congestion and Retail Business* (Washington, 1926). For the background of decentralized shopping, see J. C. Nichols, "Mistakes We Have Made in Developing Shopping Centers," Urban Land Institute, *Technical Bulletin No. 4* (August, 1945), and Boris Emmet and John E. Jeuck, *Catalogues and Counters: a History of Sears, Roebuck and Company* (Chicago, 1950).

Two histories of zoning which stress its social-control implications are Stanislaw J. Makielski, *The Politics of Zoning: The New York Experience* (New York, 1960) and Seymour I. Toll, *Zoned American* (New York, 1969). The zoning gospel can best be sampled in Edward M. Bassett, *Buildings: Their Uses and the Spaces About Them* (New York, 1931).

Finally, we should keep in mind that the suburbs are really extensions of downtown forms. Perhaps the best glimpse of the traditional "preindustrial" American town is Benjamin Franklin's *Autobiography.* The elite preserves of eastern cities are discussed in Edward Pessen, *Riches, Class, and Power before the Civil War* (Lexington, Mass., 1973), and of St. Louis, in Scott McConachie, "Public Problems and Private Places" (A revised paper first delivered at the Missouri Conference on History, May, 1970). Such fixity should be compared with the extreme geographical mobility discerned by Peter R. Knights, *The Plain People of Boston, 1830–1860: A Study in City Growth* (New York, 1971). Two fascinat-

ing discussions of metropolitan expansion divide the nine
teenth-century urban world between them: Sam Bass Warner
Jr., *The Private City, Philadelphia in Three Periods o*
Growth (Philadelphia, 1968), and Seymour J. Mandelbaum
Boss Tweed's New York (New York, 1965).

THE LURE OF THE SUBURBS
by Margaret S. Marsh and Samuel Kaplan

> *The rise of the suburbs . . .*
> *furnishes the solid basis of*
> *a hope that the evils of city*
> *life . . . may in large part be*
> *removed.*
> *Adna Weber, 1899*

AT THE TURN of this century, many reformers and planners looked to the suburbs as the hope of America and the salvation of its cities. The present numerical trend of suburbanization exceeded their wildest expectations. Today, the numbers of suburban dwellers have far outstripped the populations of the city or the farm. The 1970 census recorded a total of 76 million suburban residents, compared to 64 million urbanites and 63 million people in rural areas. However, the development of suburban America is seen as a perversion of the reformers' dream. The dichotomy between intellectual tastes and popular preferences is not new and each has lacked consistency in their approach to suburbia.

For the majority of Americans, if not for reformers and intellectuals, the lure of suburbia has been twofold. First, Americans have a fundamental antiurban bias and they have held that attitude since the earliest days of the republic. Americans are hostile to the scale, culture, and life-styles of big cities. On the other hand, there is a desire for the amenities and economic opportunities associated with urban life. Secondly, most Americans have consistently sought to live in communities with others like themselves. While our national image is one of ethnic and cultural diversity, on a community level we have tended to prefer homogeneity. However, there never have been any general rules on which groups were to be excluded. That depended on the times and the particular suburb under consideration. These attitudes, working in concert, have encouraged Americans to seek communities of like-minded residents within which to raise their families, and an environment as far removed from congested urban centers as their jobs and finances would carry them. The lure of the suburbs, therefore, is an expression of a pervasive antiurban bias in one of the most highly urbanized nations of the world, and it is an affirmation of the American commitment to homogeneity in the midst of ethnic and cultural diversity.

The manner in which these two themes merged into the twentieth-century process of suburbanization perhaps can best be explained by an examination of attitudes toward city and country that have prevailed throughout our history. In the early years of the republic, the rural life-style was considered to be the most efficacious for the maintenance of an egalitarian, democratic society. Neither city nor suburb was held in great esteem by the citizenry. The American dream was an agrarian dream, and most Americans, if asked, would probably have echoed Thomas Jefferson's view of the city (and its suburbs) as "pestilential to the morals, the health, and the liberties of man."

Despite the widespread glorification of the agrarian lifestyle, by the middle of the nineteenth century it had become clear that the path of economic opportunity led to the city. Americans loved the country but they lived, in ever-increasing numbers, in the city. Since the form and structure of the mid-nineteenth-century city was dependent on primitive transportation technology, the rich, the poor, and the middle classes all shared the same small urban space not only with each other but also with commercial and manufacturing enterprises. There is, however, no indication that urban residents liked it that way. They coped with diversity by developing an elaborate system of social segregation to accomplish the desired end of separation by race and class at a time when physical segregation was logistically impossible.

Transportation and technological innovations in the late nineteenth century not only made outlying areas more accessible but gave people freedom to decide where they would prefer to reside. Urban dwellers who could afford to began to abandon the inner city for outlying areas where they tried to create and maintain homogeneous communities in a rustic setting. They were aided in achieving their goal of homogeneity by builders who found that it was more economical, then as now, to erect homes similar to each other in style and price. Then, too, in the early years of residential decentralization, builders tended to be small businessmen who shared the values of those for whom the homes were being constructed. The homogeneity, which in the inner city had been maintained by exclusionary clubs and fraternal lodges, could now be achieved through residential segregation.

These early suburban communities needed or desired urban amenities such as sewerage facilities and fresh-water supplies. Therefore city and suburb remained in close contact. In fact, cities were able to expand and recapture suburban populations through annexation and consolidation. However, once technological advances made urban amenities possible in suburban areas, these communities invariably preferred to be isolated from the city's political domination. They instead would create a new "middle landscape," an area between city and country, or suburbia as we now call it. Technology and transportation allowed Americans to exercise their desire for residential homogeneity in a revised agrarian setting. Suburbanization did not create this desire, it simply made it possible for increasing numbers of Americans to realize it.

During the first two decades of the twentieth century, fueled by the agrarian ideal and the desire for homogeneity, suburbia continued to grow with the apparent blessing of most planners, architects, and reformers. By the time of the depression, however, many professionals had begun to closely scrutinize the phenomenon of suburbanization and concluded that it had not worked out in quite the way that they had hoped.

The New Deal presented an unprecedented opportunity for the critics of the existing suburbs to develop new alternatives. Rexford Tugwell, Director of the Resettlement Administration, urged the establishment of several thousand suburban garden cities to house families driven off the farm, as well as urban residents who wanted to escape the slums. The three thousand Greenbelt towns of which Tugwell had dreamed were cut to twenty-five in the Administration's proposal to Congress, then to three by Congress itself. (The three were Greenbelt, Maryland, near Washington, D.C.; Greendale, Wisconsin, near Milwaukee; and Greenhills, Ohio, near Cincinnati.)

The sharp reduction of the numbers of towns to be built did not diminish the enthusiasm of the program's supporters. The Greenbelt Town idea was still seen as the best way to create the ideal suburb. The architects and planners, among the most celebrated in their professions, were committed to creating complete communities, on the model of Ebenezer Howard's Garden Cities of an earlier era. Yet when given their chance, the experts showed little innovation in the face of politics and the profit motive. With the exception of Greenbelt, no provisions were made for diversity of population; the architects designed homes for young couples with one or two children. The development of a "complete community" was impossible without older people, single men and women, large families, or childless couples. The rules for acceptance into the communities reinforced the ideas built into the houses. In Greenbelt, a wife who worked was an automatic reason for rejection. Blacks were excluded from all Greenbelt towns, and the economic restrictions limited prospective residents to a specific income level. The towns either discouraged, or prohibited outright, the development of industries, making it inevitable that they would become dormitory communities. As a result, the one formal effort that had been made to redirect the process of suburbanization had simply consolidated the set of trends already in progress.

Although the New Deal planners failed to alter America's suburban priorities, they retained a vision of suburbia which combined the advantages of city and country in well-planned, self-contained communities serving a cross-section of ages and classes. The lure of suburbia for planners and reformers was nothing less than to create a new American environment. Yet by the early 1950s, their dream seemed to be in shreds. The post-World War II era witnessed what might be called the greatest land rush in our history. Family life had been stunted for nearly two decades—first by depression, then by war. Returning veterans, anxious to make up for so much lost time, started families at an unprecedented rate. It was called the "baby boom." The fact that cities did not have enough space for all the new families only reinforced the suburban preference of most people.

Residential construction, no longer limited by wartime restrictions, quickly filled the gap. New mass-production construction techniques, pioneered by the Levitts but soon taken up by other developers, facilitated the creation of complete "packaged" suburbs on large tracts of land at comparatively low cost. Former potato fields suddenly became suburban communities with hundreds of homes. Easy financing, offered by the Veterans Administration and the Federal Housing Administration, combined with the relatively inexpensive prices of many new homes, encouraged millions of additional Americans to leave the cities for a little space of their own in the suburbs.

Overall, the families who moved out to the suburbs in the late forties and early fifties seemed reasonably satisfied with their new environment. They owned their own homes, which is a prime part of the lure of suburbia, and had a little open space for the children to play. But if the suburbs pleased most of the residents, they did not please the planners, who saw their vision of a new American environment disintegrate into a nightmarish scene of "little boxes made of ticky tacky"—to quote Malvina Reynolds' satiric tune. Lewis Mumford, in *The*

City in History, expressed the frustrations of those who had such hopes for the suburbs:

> While the suburb served only a favored minority, it neither spoiled the countryside nor threatened the city. But now that the drift to the outer ring (sparked by the twin elements of popularity and horsepower and spurred by government housing loans) has become a mass movement, it tends to destroy the value of both environments without producing anything but a dreary substitute, devoid of form and even more devoid of the original suburban values.

Reformers, social commentators and intellectuals generally shared Mumford's view. The people had despoiled the one place left to rebuild America. There was no frontier left, the cities were overbuilt and unplanned, and rural areas were rapidly receding. Intellectuals now attacked suburbia with a fury which knew no bounds. It was not just the physical shape of suburbia or the exclusionary practices of communities which they excoriated but the people themselves. This moral rage can be seen in the literature of the era. In *The Crack in the Picture Window,* a modern morality tale about the evils of the suburbs, John Keats called his principal characters John and Mary Drone. Short on subtlety and long on indictment, his criticisms did have some validity, especially when they focused on the haphazard and unplanned physical attributes of the postwar developments. Keats, however, did not direct his most heated invective toward the houses or toward their builders, but against the people who lived in them. He was convinced that "the dwelling shapes the dweller. When all dwellings are the same shape, all dwellers are the same shape." Other factors, such as childhood experiences, ethnic or class background, and education, were irrelevant. One wonders if Keats would have similarly stereotyped the residents of a city block of brownstones.

Diatribes like *The Crack in the Picture Window* may seem excessive now; but they represented a widely held journalistic and intellectual perception of the suburbs in the fifties. While the rhetoric of other analysts was somewhat more subdued, the image of suburbia remained uniformly negative. Critics of the suburbs castigated its supposedly matriarchal character: a community dominated by women was no place to raise little boys who needed suitable masculine images. Family life apparently suffered in other ways as well. Suburban ennui led inevitably to sexual excess; the media seized on stories of call-girl rings composed of housewives, and of wife-swapping parties that seemed to be a staple entertainment in suburbia. Suburbanites drank too much and were too hungry for status. They ruined their own lives, then forced their children into the same competitive mold. Privacy, individualism, the stimulation of cultural and intellectual activities were strangers to the suburbia that the social commentators created.

Apparently it did not occur to them that they blamed the suburbs for all the elements that cosmopolitan Americans found stifling in American culture as a whole: the mediocrity of popular tastes; family-centeredness; consensus political attitudes; and social conformity. Aside from despoiling the land, the suburban explosion coincided with the emergence of a popular culture dominated by the mass media and the critics turned on suburbia as scapegoat. By the mid-fifties no self-respecting intellectual would venture a kind word about the suburbs—even if he lived in one. The suburbs, within a span of a half century, had gone from a position as the hope of modern civilization to the cause of its undoing in the eyes of reformers and intellectuals. Such a radical transformation in the image of suburbia immediately raises two questions. Were the suburbs really as dismal as the critics claimed? If so, why did millions of Americans continue to flock to them?

The answer to these questions is not very complicated. Quite simply, the majority of suburbanites did not view the suburbs in the same light as the intellectuals, who have always been critical of popular tastes. Most residents of even the "ticky tacky" tract houses, while not totally satisfied with a home that looked like every other house on the block, felt that they had achieved certain limited goals. The critics, on the other hand, were unable to accept the fact that the American family could be content with so little.

The extreme divergence between the popular and intellectual perceptions of suburbia eventually led scholars to question the validity of some of the criticisms. By the early sixties, unrestrained outbursts against the "suburban way of life" had begun to give way to serious academic inquiry. Suburbs were analyzed from every conceivable perspective: demographic, ecological, political, psychological, sociological, religious, and economic. If the studies agreed on any one point, it was that the "real" suburbia defied stereotyping. While urban journalists claimed that it was virtually impossible to distinguish one suburb from another, the social scientists discovered that the "typical suburb" simply did not exist. Upper-middle-class suburbs differed markedly from working-class communities, and those of the lower middle class from the other two. Black suburbs were like neither all-white nor racially integrated ones.

The first communities to be studied extensively by the social scientists were those of the upper middle class, which housed professionals and rising corporate executives. Some of the studies seemed to affirm the complaints voiced by the critics. In *Crestwood Heights* (a pseudonym for a suburb of Toronto), the residents were upwardly mobile families, very conscious of status, who destroyed old friendships as they became more successful. The men were ambitious and totally career-oriented. The wives did not usually hold jobs; they devoted themselves to home and family. The families of *Crestwood Heights* were, to use terms originating with sociologist Herbert Gans, child-centered and adult-directed, which means that the parents have specific goals for their children and provide direction toward those goals. Children were pressured to excel in school in order to gain admission to a prestigious university. Like the adults, they led rather rigidly scheduled lives—ballet or piano lessons, scouts, and summer camp. Despite the regimentation and striving, however, most residents seemed fairly content. The authors of *Crestwood Heights* discovered no more than the expected proportion of mental pathology or dissatisfaction. There are problems, to be sure, in a life-style based on material goals and status-seeking, but these are problems not merely of suburbia, but of upper-middle-class executives and their families in general.

As suburban studies began to focus on other groups besides the "organization men" and their families, it became clearer to analysts that the criticism directed at suburbia was really concerned with the life-styles of particular classes. Bennett Berger's *Working-Class Suburb* effectively challenged the myth of a monolithic suburbia. It was true that the auto workers who relocated in the suburbs did experience some changes in their lives as a result of the move. Many acquired new friends, a heightened feeling of respectability, and a greater interest in politics. Still, they never developed those characteristics considered the most important attributes of a suburban life-style. Families in the working-class suburb did not involve themselves in the rich associational life that supposedly dominates suburbia; neither did they develop a child-oriented perspective. Unlike the parents of *Crestwood Heights*, working-class parents did not pressure their children to be upwardly mobile, nor did they center their lives around them. Berger found "little evidence of pronounced striving, status anxiety, or orientation to the future. [The auto workers] neither give parties nor go to them. Their tastes and preferences seem untouched by the images of 'suburbia' portrayed in the mass media." Certainly there was little congruence between the upper-middle-class suburbs so extensively studied in the fifties and Berger's *Working-Class Suburb*.

Herbert Gans' *The Levittowners* has provided social scientists with the most sympathetic account of suburbia to date. Levittown, New Jersey (near Philadelphia), was still under construction when Gans moved in to begin his participant-observer study of community formation in this lower-middle-class suburb. He discovered that very little of the boredom which is supposed to be characteristic of suburbia existed in Levittown. Residents enjoyed their houses, yards, and the company of compatible neighbors. While the community did have problems—personal disorganization, family difficulties, inability to cope with community conflict—Gans suggested that by and large these are the problems of lower-middle-class America, not of the suburbs per se. Gans castigated the critics of suburbia for their "ethnocentrism" and insisted that the value system of self-conscious cosmopolitans should not be forced on the rest of society. He concluded that "whatever its imperfections, Levittown is a good place to live." While Gans had criticisms of his own of the inequities of suburbanization—particularly of the refusal of communities to open their door to the poor and minority members of the society—he did not wish to halt the process. Rather, he contended that suburban living should be made available to those who were excluded.

Other observers, whatever their own personal preferences, agreed that for the most part people liked living in the suburbs. Most suburbanites declared that wherever they came from—the cities, the farms, the older suburbs—they considered their lives better where they were now living. Few contemplated a return to the farm or city, especially not to the city. As Scott Donaldson noted in *The Suburban Myth*:

> The overwhelming majority of people who live in rows of identical little boxes brought a . . . limited dream with them from the city: a little open country, a little fresh air, at a price they could afford. It is a dream they think they have realized. Whose duty is it to disillusion them?

A study conducted by the suburban newspaper, *Newsday* (which serves Long Island, New York), in the early seventies corroborates Donaldson's viewpoint. About 90 per cent of those interviewed said that they "would recommend their present communities to friends as a place to live." They indicated that on the whole they were quite satisfied with suburbia, even though it might not have lived up to all their dreams. Only 21 per cent said that they were bothered because "not enough different kinds of people live here." The survey, in short, showed that most people want to live where they feel comfortable, and suburbia meets that need for increasing numbers of Americans.

The migration of people seeking the "limited dream"

swelled to remarkable proportions during the sixties. Between 1960 and 1970 the nation's population increased by about 12 per cent, to approximately 205 million. Nearly 75 per cent of that growth occurred in the suburbs. Altogether, the country's twenty-five largest cities gained only 710,000 persons, while their suburban areas increased by 8.9 million. Clearly the United States is progressing from a nation of cities to a nation of suburbs.

Until the 1960s, whatever their social class, suburbanites were usually at a similar life-cycle stage: married and raising a family. However, now the suburban lure was beckoning those groups which had traditionally preferred city life—singles, the elderly, and childless couples. The reasons these groups started to move to suburbia seem to be twofold: The positive attraction of suburbia and an increased fear of the city. Urban riots, racial unrest, excessive taxation, pollution, and crime dominated the litany of complaints about the city. Older neighborhoods in the outer city which were as homogeneous as suburbia had begun to change. Many elderly residents therefore decided to join their children in the suburbs. Those older suburban residents whose children had grown up did not return to the city but stayed in suburban areas.

Many young married couples delayed having families until they were already settled in the suburbs. Those children who had grown up in suburbia seemed satisfied enough to stay and they were joined by a new influx of single persons from the city. However, the increased lure was changing the very nature and landscape of suburban areas. Since many people did not want or could not afford single-family detached houses, there was a marked increase in the number of apartment houses, condominiums, and garden apartments built in suburbia. Homogeneity was still retained in part by preference and design. Retirement villages in suburbia were for the elderly, while singles along with many young married couples tended to prefer housing complexes designed for their age groups.

Other groups of people also were beginning to become aware of the lure of suburbia—the poor and the blacks of large cities. There always had been poor people in suburbia and there always have been some black suburbs. Blacks with adequate economic resources had been moving to suburbia for years. But for an overwhelming number of blacks and poor people, the cities of America were called home.

Federal and state authorities traditionally linked these "underprivileged" groups with the cities through such policies as urban renewal. However, there is little evidence that they preferred city life. After all, members of these groups were the ones who were the most frequently victimized by crime and relegated to the worse areas of the city. In addition, the level of expectation has risen, thanks to mass media, the civil rights crusade, and the promises of the Great Society. These groups now have begun to focus on a new promised land—suburbia. The NAACP and organizations such as Suburban Action Institute have been the champions of their right to move into the suburbs. However, for the most part, the lure of suburbia for these groups is not a homogeneous community but a pastoral vision of better living conditions outside the city.

Corporations also started to re-examine their commitments to the city and many of them have decided to relocate in suburbia. Of course, the suburbs had not been devoid of business enterprises before the 1960s. Some suburbs were almost completely industrial since their original development, and even residential communities had always needed shopping centers and service industries. But the large-scale move of corporate headquarters, research and development companies, and light manufacturing into primarily residential suburbs is a new phenomenon. One of the principal forces behind the corporate movement is the encouragement of the suburbanites themselves, who find the potential tax revenue from "clean" industry and offices almost irresistible. Advertisements appear in the *Wall Street Journal* and the New York *Times* designed to entice the commutation-weary executive: "Join the Great Corporate Getaway to Connecticut" . . . or New Jersey, Long Island, and Westchester County.

Many corporations react to such proposals enthusiastically, citing lower taxes, cheaper land, and fewer commuting problems as some of the reasons for their relocation. There also are other, less tangible benefits. In a very real sense, the lure of the suburbs for the corporations is similar to its lure for individuals. Richard Aszling, Vice-President for Public Relations for General Foods, one of the first companies to leave New York City, explained one aspect of his firm's attraction to the suburbs: "We were darn near lost in New York. Here [White Plains, N.Y.] we are an important part of the community." Today the residential suburb has become almost as much a place to work as it is to live. While the overall numbers of jobs in all categories still remains greater in the cities, the trend is toward more jobs in the suburbs. In the latter half of the 1960s, the central cities of the nation's forty largest metropolitan areas gained 782,000 jobs. During the same period, the suburbs of those metropolitan areas gained 4,370,000 jobs—85 per cent of the increase.

The dramatic growth of the suburbs, particularly in terms of apartment dwellers and corporations, has begun to prompt fears of overcrowding and worries about the future of suburbia. Added to the demands of low-income and minority groups, as well as the environmental consciousness of the 1970s, continued massive growth has provoked considerable controversy over the way in which new development should be handled. The power to control and shape growth has, since the early twentieth century, rested in the zoning laws. But because of overlapping jurisdictions, aggravated by unequal tax burdens, suburban communities have been unable to work together in metropolitan areas to map and carry out rational land-use plans. The communities are little islands, each zealously guarding their zoning powers.

Planners shudder at the chaos without adequately understanding it. They point to the remarkable disorganization of Orange County, California, the largest all-suburban county in the country. As Los Angeles sprawled southward during the sixties, the county population doubled to 1.4 million, and its 25 municipalities and 133 self-governing districts scrambled to

annex every piece of taxable land in sight. Little consideration
was given to siting, or to the relationships of residential, industrial, or commercial developments. The result was a crazy-
quilt pattern of roads and boundaries, creating a garish tan-
gle and a host of problems. Chicago's metropolitan area is in
a similar confused state, with 1,113 local governments. Nassau County, Long Island (a suburb of New York City),
contains two cities, three townships, sixty-four villages, and
280 "special districts" (for fire, water, education, police protection, etc.). Suffolk County, which comprises the rest of
Long Island, consists of ten townships, twenty-eight incorporated villages, and 527 special districts. The 2.6 million people on Long Island are thus served by 914 separate governments.

The multiplicity of governmental and jurisdictional units
has rendered rational planning on a metropolitan scale all but
impossible. Planners have likened the political conditions of
the suburbs to that of the Balkan States at the turn of the century. But while the advocates of regional planning despair
over the situation, many suburban residents prefer their governmental units to be small and independent. They view their
local governments as the heirs of nineteenth-century small-
town democracy in the United States, and have no desire to
relinquish control of their communities. This attitude is
strengthened by the fact that many suburbanites left the city
with a conviction that large-scale government was impersonal
and excessively bureaucratic in nature.

There is some indication that the arguments of the suburban residents have a measure of validity. While many urban
specialists continue to maintain that the only rational way to
govern the suburbs is through centralization and regionaliza-
tion, the contention is often precisely the opposite when the
city comes under discussion. Cities are now trying to compete
with the lure of the suburbs by duplicating some of its most
attractive features. Community school boards, neighborhood
councils, and other elements of government decentralization
are frequently urged as partial solutions to the problems of
urban government. Cities also are building suburbanlike shop-

ping plazas and new towns within their boundaries. Mayor Richard Daley of Chicago summed it up recently when he said, "We hope and we can make city life the same as life in the suburbs."

Planners have exhibited a degree of humility in the face of our urban crisis. Some now admit that there had been too much planning from above without consulting the residents of urban areas about to be renovated. Therefore, advocacy planning has come into vogue. This approach attempts to allow neighborhood residents to become involved in the planning process. However, when many of the same experts focus their attention on the suburbs, they contend that the wishes of the local community must be disregarded in favor of professional judgments which would "benefit" the entire region. Such inconsistencies only serve to heighten suburban hostility toward regional planning.

Besides skepticism about the efficacy of big government and centralized planning, there is another factor that militates against regional co-operation. Most Americans, urban and suburban alike, tend to be oriented toward their homes and families. As homeowners, suburbanites are very concerned about anything that threatens their "investment." They believe that the small municipality offers the best hope of insuring the value of that investment. Difficulties arise because the tendency is for homeowners to equate the preservation of the status quo with the protection of their property. This in turn leads directly to one of the most serious, and valid, criticisms of suburbia: the resistance to open communities to other groups, particularly racial minorities, lower-income families, and senior citizens.

In itself such insularity is not a peculiarly suburban attitude. Americans since the eighteenth century have viewed land as a commodity rather than a social resource, and so have been primarily interested in maintaining property values in their own communities by keeping out those who might adversely affect them. The outlying areas of many cities, which resemble suburbs in their scale, homogeneous population, and degree of home ownership, were not able to protect their way of life from encroachment because they were part of the larger city. Perhaps suburbs will be equally unsuccessful but it is generally believed that change is inhibited by the existence of smaller political units which are more responsive to residents' demands.

Zoning has served as an effective inhibitor of the encroachment of "undesirables" throughout the twentieth century, but it has become doubtful that the zoning shield will continue to insure residential homogeneity. In the spring of 1975, two major court decisions challenged the inviolability of zoning. The first came in New Jersey, where the State Supreme Court ruled that it was inherently discriminatory for suburban towns not to make provisions for low- and moderate-income developments. Later that year, the Court of Appeals of New York also struck at exclusionary practices, ruling that nonresidents have the right to challenge the use of federal funds in those communities that zone against minorities and lower-income groups. While it is too early to tell what the full impact of these decisions will be, the direction of the rulings is to clearly support the rights of low- and moderate-income families to have affordable housing made available in the suburbs. If they are sustained, the effect should be to create a more heterogeneous population mix within individual communities.

The truth is that the lure of suburbia has literally affected every aspect of American society. The more affluent members of society who first moved there resented middle-class groups seeking a "limited dream." These middle-class groups could not afford anything more than a mass-produced colonial, ranch, or Cape Cod house in a tract development. The bourgeois tastes of these suburban areas were scorned by all but those who lived there and the lower classes and minority groups who were excluded. For many intellectuals, reformers and social critics, the lure of suburbia was a mandate to build a new America in the middle landscape. They were furious that their garden spot had been overrun by popular tastes. Somehow they had mentally reserved suburbia for social experimentation and planned unit developments without understanding the limitations of planning in a democratic society.

Naturally, the lure of suburbia has affected cities which now find themselves in direct competition with their suburban neighbors. Aside from rooting for the energy crisis and publicizing increased suburban crime rates, they have been forced to copy traditional modes of suburban life within the inner city. Actually the suburban competition may make cities better places to live. The poor and minority members of society want a part of the suburban dream. Their entry into suburbia has been the most difficult but their desire is not hard to understand.

The original lure of suburbia was a desire for a homogeneous community within an agrarian setting. This is as true today as it was in 1870. However, as each new group moved to suburban areas they were forced to modify their dream to some extent. The desire for urban amenities meant giving up or revising the agrarian setting. Homogeneous communities were achieved but suburbia today generally is as heterogeneous as any city. Blue-collar and white-collar workers, blacks, and professionals all know which suburban communities share their values and tend to move into those areas. The conflict arises when certain groups cannot afford to move into suburban communities or are excluded. However, integration by race and class always has proven to be a difficult problem and is not unique to suburbia.

Since suburbia is viewed as a haven from modern urban life, efficiency has not been an important criterion in its formation. One easily can prove that single-family houses and small governmental units are wasteful and inefficient. Yet these arguments have had little impact on the persons seeking the suburban dream. For the bureaucratic ideal of efficiency has usually been achieved at the expense of organic social relationships and a sense of community.

Yet suburbanites have been tempted to accept change to some degree. Since their children cannot afford single-family detached houses, they have reluctantly been accepting forms of multifamily housing. Although smaller in scale, these housing units will change the nature of suburban life. Similarly, the temptation of increasing a community's tax base has led to an acceptance of business and industry. Although built on rustic campuses and usually "clean," this development also will alter suburbia. Other changes are being imposed on suburban communities by the courts as indicated by recent judicial decisions in New Jersey and New York.

Americans in general do not view suburbia as a failure but as a bright success. Its lure is now universal and perhaps popularity is its greatest problem. For the more dense and diverse its population and economic base becomes, the more the original lure will be destroyed. This paradox is not easily solved but Americans probably will continue to seek their dreams in suburbia, whether or not the reality belies them.

BIBLIOGRAPHY

IT IS IMPOSSIBLE to understand the process of suburbanization or the communities formed in suburbia without some understanding of the city itself. Adna Weber, *Nineteenth Century Cities* (New York, 1899), one of the first statistical analyses of the process of urbanization, contains an eloquent plea for the development of suburbs to cure the evils of the cities. For an extensive review of urban development as a whole, consult Lewis Mumford, *The City in History* (New York, 1961). Sam Bass Warner, *The Urban Wilderness* (New York, 1972) has written an excellent critique of the urban process in the United States. Especially provocative is his analysis of the American attitude toward property and its impact on growth.

On early suburbanization see Harlan Douglass, *The Suburban Trend* (New York, 1925), a discussion of diverse suburban forms in an ecological perspective. Douglass is representative of a generation who saw the suburbs as the best hope for creating a "middle landscape" between city and country. Sam Bass Warner, *Streetcar Suburbs* (Cambridge, Mass., 1962) offers an in-depth study of nineteenth-century suburbanization. Kenneth Jackson's "Metropolitan Politics vs.

Suburban Autonomy: Politics on the Crabgrass Frontier," in Kenneth Jackson and Stanley Schultz, eds., *Cities in American History* (New York, 1972) contains a good description of working- and lower-class suburbs in the nineteenth century. The Greenbelt towns are given thorough and detailed coverage in Joseph Arnold, *The New Deal in the Suburbs* (Columbus, Ohio, 1971), an excellent analysis of the limitations of planning in a democratic society.

Criticism of the suburbs and their ways of life first became important after mass residential decentralization began in the late 1940s and early 1950s. The most vicious and least subtle attack may be found in John Keats, *The Crack in the Picture Window* (Boston, 1956). Keats ascribes all the social problems of mass society to the fact that people live in suburbs and reveals an ill-disguised longing for the past. Richard E. Gordon, et al., *The Split-Level Trap* (New York, 1962) uses isolated case studies to "prove" that suburbia is an incubator for severe mental pathology. A. G. Spectorsky's *The Exurbanites* (New York, 1955) is a very popular, well-written, and generally critical study of the way of life of some of America's most affluent suburban dwellers. On the perils of growing up in the suburbs, see Peter Wyden's *Suburbia's Coddled Kids* (New York, 1962), which suggests that it is possible, though difficult, for children of the affluent society to become mature, responsible adults. Journalistic commentary during the fifties was predominantly negative. Random perusing of popular magazines, including issues of *Time, Look,* and *Newsweek* published during the fifties, will yield extensive information on the media attitude toward suburbia.

Among the more serious studies, possibly the most influential indictment of the suburbs appears in a book as much about corporations as it is about suburbs: William H. Whyte, *The Organization Man* (New York, 1956). Whyte argues that the corporation and its organization men who live in the suburbs have destroyed American individualism. A somewhat more optimistic interpretation is John Seely et al., *Crestwood Heights* (New York, 1956), a case study of an upper-middle-class suburb of Toronto; although not a negative portrayal, it gives some credence to the antisuburban point of view, especially regarding conformity and status-seeking.

Two of the best analyses of suburban life and culture are Bennett Berger, *Working-Class Suburb* (Berkeley, Calif., 1960) and Herbert Gans, *The Levittowners: Ways of Life and Politics in a New Suburban Community* (New York, 1967). The former is the first sociological study to concentrate on working-class suburbanites. One of its best chapters debunks what Berger refers to as "the myth of suburbia." Gans's participant-observer study of community formation in Levittown, New Jersey, is one of the most sophisticated commentaries on suburbia to date. Gans discovered that the move to the suburbs does not change the life-styles or expectations of its residents, except insofar as changes are desired and anticipated prior to the move. For a briefer discussion of Gans's point of view, see his "Urbanism and Suburbanism as Ways of Life: a Re-evaluation of Definitions," in Arnold Rose, ed., *Human Behavior and Social Process: an Interactionist Approach* (Boston, 1962), pp. 626–48.

William Dobriner, *Class in Suburbia* (Englewood Cliffs, N.J., 1963) examines several different suburbs and concludes that the differences among them can be explained by economic and social class. Dobriner also has edited a book on the suburbs, *The Suburban Community* (New York, 1958) which is one of the most comprehensive general introductions to the findings of suburban analysts during the 1950s. An important defense of the suburbs and their ways of life is Scott Donaldson, *The Suburban Myth* (New York, 1969), a critique of the antisuburban perspective. Especially valuable is his treatment of the critics as frustrated Jeffersonian agrarian idealists. In addition to Donaldson's treatment of the pastoral myths which have heavily influenced the American perspective of suburbia, two excellent books confront the more general issue of American antiurban attitudes. Lucia and Morton White, in *The Intellectual vs. the City* (Cambridge, Mass., 1962) discuss the philosophical bases of antiurbanism. Peter Schmitt, in *Back to Nature: the Arcadian Myth in*

Urban America (New York, 1969) argues that the agrarian myth had disappeared by the late nineteenth century. The advocates of the "back to nature" movement of that era, he contends, did not desire the eradication of the city; they wanted instead for Americans to unite their urban consciousness with a pastoral sensibility.

On the growing popularity of apartment living in the suburbs, see Max Neutze, *The Suburban Apartment Boom* (Baltimore, 1968). The best place to look for information on the corporate movement to suburbia is the financial section of the New York *Times*. The movement to open suburbia to poor and minority members of society is examined in Linda and Paul Davidoff and Neil N. Gold, "The Suburbs Have to Open Their Gates," New York *Times Magazine*, November 7, 1971.

We have not concentrated on the politics of suburbia in this essay, except as it relates to the reasons that people tolerate and even approve of the inefficient multiplicity of governmental units. For a decidedly negative assessment of this phenomenon, see Robert C. Wood, *Suburbia: Its People and their Politics* (Boston, 1959). Wood argues that no rational justification exists for the continued political autonomy of the suburbs. A more positive viewpoint may be found in Frederick M. Wirt et al., *On the City's Rim: Politics and Policy in Suburbia* (Lexington, Mass., 1972), which also includes a comprehensive summary of suburban growth.

Finally, we should mention some of the prescriptions for coping with the problems of suburbanization. William H. Whyte, who has mellowed somewhat in his view of the suburbs since the fifties, suggests practical and workable methods for improving the quality of life without destroying suburbia itself, in *The Last Landscape* (New York, 1968). Melvin Webber, "Order in Diversity: Community Without Propinquity" in Lowdon Wingo, ed., *Cities and Space* (Baltimore, 1964), claims that modern community formation has resulted in an unprecedented opportunity for Americans to reaffirm their traditions of freedom, individualism, and social mobility. He also provides detailed suggestions for the implementation of that potential. Samuel Kaplan, *The Dream Deferred: People, Politics and Planning in Suburbia* (New York, 1976) is a more personal analysis of suburban development.

THE IMPACT OF SUBURBANIZATION ON GOVERNMENT AND POLITICS IN CONTEMPORARY AMERICA
by Pierce B. Wilkinson

FOR OVER ONE HUNDRED YEARS Americans have been leaving the farms with their rural way of life and moving to the cities. Immigrants swelled the urban population as well. The 1920 census registered the critical change of our population from predominantly rural to urban. During much of this time, however, another demographic pattern was emerging, though rarely noticed or remarked upon at the time. In part this second pattern was a function of the first: the urban growth centers were expanding rapidly on their fringes, frequently beyond their municipal boundaries. Between 1900 and 1940 the suburban population almost doubled from 8.2 million to 15.6 million. Following World War II this trend dramatically increased so that by 1970 more Americans lived in suburbs than lived in either the central cities or in the rural areas. Projections indicate that these trends will continue: at least for the near future, rural and urban population will decline proportionately while the suburban population will increase. All major demographic movements are accompanied by social, economic, cultural, and political change. The purpose of this article is to examine the impact of suburbanization on our governmental and political processes.

In a democratic republic there is a fundamental assumption that the people will have some impact on the key govern-

mental decisions affecting their lives. Practical concerns arise
as to how that input should be accomplished. An electoral
system goes a long way toward that goal; but questions of equity arise regarding the relative political impact of people living in different areas. When people relocate in large numbers,
will that affect the democratic input system; will it affect the
outputs of the political system? In short, what has happened
to the political and governmental system as a result of recent
suburbanization? There are several aspects of the question
that deserve attention. First, in the race for the presidency,
that most visible election in the American system, has suburbanization had any impact upon campaign strategy and its
outcome? Secondly, how has suburbanization affected the
Congress? To what extent has the tremendous surge in population during the 1960s affected representative patterns and to
what extent has it affected legislative politics and outputs?
Third, what impact has suburbanization had upon state politics and government? Fourth, has the recent population shift
favored one or another of our two political parties? Fifth,
what effect has the trend toward suburbanization had upon
governmental policies?

THE PRESIDENCY

Since the presidential election is closely tied to the popular
vote, where the voters live and vote is likely to have an impact upon campaign strategy. The basic demographic pattern
described above has resulted in a continuing shift of votes
from inner cities to the suburbs. In Figure 1, adapted from
the suggested Republican campaign strategy of Kevin Phillips,
author of *The Emerging Republican Majority*, we see a distinct pattern in presidential voting developed over the period
from 1928 to 1972. Based on elections in the New York City
area which is the largest Standard Metropolitan Statistical
Area (SMSA) in the country, it shows the relative decline
of inner-city votes for President compared with the suburban
vote. Furthermore, this graph includes only the older, closer,
and in-state suburbs of New York City. If the newer and out-

FIGURE 1

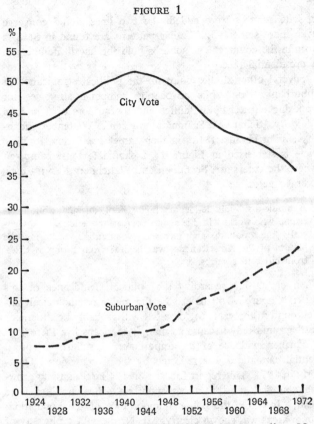

City v. *Suburbs*: Presidential Elections in Metropolitan New York, 1924–1972

SOURCES: Adapted from K. Phillips, *The Emerging Republican Majority* (New York, 1970) and the New York *Times* November 9, 1972.

——Percentage of total New York State vote cast within New York City

— —Percentage of total New York State vote cast by major suburban counties

of-state suburbs were added, the two lines would converge even more since 1952. Similar patterns are found in SMSAs around the country. The suburbs hold the key to numbers in a presidential race.

Several other studies point up the political significance of suburbanization. While advocating campaign strategies for opposing parties, both Phillips and the authors of *The Real Majority*, Richard M. Scammon and Ben J. Wattenberg, identify similar characteristics in their target population. Phillips' view is suggested in Figure 1: a candidate must campaign where the voters are. Scammon and Wattenberg identify their average voter as:

A middle-aged, middle-income, high-school educated, white Protestant, who works with his hands, decreasingly ethnic. . . . Generally metropolitan, and increasingly suburban, following the pattern of the American postwar hegira: from farms to cities, from cities to suburbs.

Their conclusion regarding the political significance of this shift: "Suburbia will indeed be the major psephological battleground in the years to come but will probably be the major battleground only because so many Americans live there."

Further evidence of the importance of suburbs to presidential candidates was reported by the Congressional Quarterly in 1971. This report focused on 194 large, rapidly growing counties, most of them suburban. Their findings were clear, "In 1968, the political importance of the population-boom areas was shown clearly. Mr. Nixon built a plurality of more than 1.6 million votes in the 194 counties, more than three times his nationwide plurality of 510,315 votes." A shift of votes in suburbia and Hubert Humphrey might have been President.

The continuing impact of these rapidly growing counties has special importance for presidential elections. These counties cast more than one third of the 1968 presidential vote in eleven states. These eleven states accounted for 131 out of 538 electoral votes. A solid suburban vote would put any candidate well on the way to the constitutionally required majority of 270 electoral votes.

Politicians themselves are well aware of these implications and it is evident that candidates of both parties recognize the significance of this voting bloc. While searching for a new Republican majority to challenge the Democratic coalition forged in the 1930s and 1940s, party leaders turned their attention to the suburbs. Thomas E. Dewey, the Republican presidential candidate, had won 56 per cent of the suburbs in the twelve largest non-southern cities in 1948. Dwight D. Eisenhower was able to campaign vigorously in these areas and raise the level to 61 per cent in 1952 and 63 per cent in 1956. Not only was the percentage growing but the population in these areas was increasing also: a boon to the Republicans in those years; undoubtedly an area to be cultivated by future Republican candidates.

In 1972 the so-called "Southern Strategy" of the Nixon campaign team included working on this potential voter source. While denying that Phillips' book on campaign strategy affected the candidate's actual plans there were remarkable similarities between them. In both, the suburbs were prime targets. The result was an incredible Nixon majority of 70 per cent. This phenomenon was in part vitiated by the fact that the national trend also was so overwhelming that the significance of the suburban vote and trend is problematic. Republican candidates undoubtedly aimed for these votes, however.

But the suburbs had become a target area for Democratic presidential aspirants as well. In 1960 John F. Kennedy decided the suburbs were not necessarily Republican but were merely affected by the Eisenhower euphoria of the 1950s. He decided in October to devote a major portion of his remaining resources to the suburbs, focusing on younger voters especially. During the last days of this close and toughly fought campaign, suburbia was seen as the key to the election. President Eisenhower was brought out to work the suburbs of Philadelphia and Cleveland while Kennedy campaigned in the fringes of New York and Philadelphia.

An analysis of the suburban vote in that election showed a Democrat could make inroads. Kennedy broke even or won a slight majority in the inner suburbs of the large SMSAs outside the South. He was able to reduce the overall Republican share of the suburban vote to 52 per cent, thereby securing the necessary margin for victory. Nixon had retained the outer suburbs for the Republicans, but this was not enough to win the election. The Johnson landslide of 1964 again showed that the suburbs were electoral battlefields not to be conceded to either party, although Republicans usually fare better there. Goldwater, an unpopular candidate within his own party, garnered only 40 per cent of the suburban vote demonstrating the fluidity of the party vote in suburbia.

Presidential campaigns have been significantly affected by the patterns of suburbanization, therefore. A candidate must address himself to those voters since they might provide the margin necessary for victory. Neither major party can afford to write them off since they are the single largest geographical bloc in the nation. Their statistical importance is even more obvious in the more populous states with large numbers of electoral votes. Specialists like Scammon, Wattenberg, and Phillips as well as the campaign patterns of recent political candidates testify to the importance of this portion of the electorate in planning campaign strategy. Yet their importance is still a function of sheer numbers combined with location. There is little evidence that they form a unique voting bloc within the American electorate in presidential elections.

THE CONGRESS

Since elections to Congress involve a different process than the presidency, the impact of suburbanization must be viewed from another perspective. Population shifts will affect the Senate least of all since each state is guaranteed two seats and both are elected at large. The impact of suburbanization would be seen in the campaign patterns within the state and would differ from state to state depending upon the degree of suburbanization.

The House of Representatives, however, is directly tied to population, and shifts in population should be reflected in redistricting and reapportionment. Therefore, the impact of suburbanization should be more clearly visible. The history of state action in redistricting, however, has not been a bright one. Rather, years of inactivity had resulted in badly malapportioned congressional districts. As the population figures show, people were moving from rural areas to urban centers; but state legislatures were reluctant to redistrict their apportioned House seats. This resulted in a rural, usually conservative, bias thoroughly unrepresentative of the urbanized American people as well as in districts of wildly unequal population. New York's largest district had nine times as many people as its smallest district in the early 1930s. In the 1940s Illinois had a variance of 800 per cent between its smallest and largest district. In 1961 California had 588,933 in its largest district and 301,872 in its smallest. Such inequalities were not uncommon throughout the country.

During most of the twentieth century it was the cities that suffered the burdens of these inequities. Accordingly, urban interests challenged the situation in state legislatures, state courts, and Congress but with little success. Even the federal courts concluded in *Colgrove* v. *Green* (1946) that the issue was a "political thicket" into which the courts should not wander. All along, the struggle was envisioned as a rural-urban split.

However, the census of 1950 showed a staggering shift in population to the suburbs. This meant any successful challenge to the prorural districting schemes in congressional seats would benefit the suburbs at least as much as the central cities. The tide turned in 1962 with the case of *Baker* v. *Carr*, brought to the Supreme Court by urban voters in Tennessee. While specifically concerned with similar prorural malapportionment in the state legislature, the case had wider significance. It opened the court doors to apportionment and districting cases, reversing the "political thicket" views of the earlier Court. In rapid succession the Supreme Court applied its powers to several states' congressional districts. *Wesberry*

v. *Sanders* (1964) established the necessity for substantial equality in population for House districts. Other cases had similar effect and by the late 1960s inequality in size had been largely eliminated. *Kirkpatrick* v. *Preisler* (1969) disallowed any numerical variance between districts without specific justification.

The combination of these court cases, state redistricting, and the changing population resulted in a dramatic but deserved shift in representation patterns. As shown in Figure 2, which charts those districts that fit clearly into either rural, urban, or suburban categories, from 1962 to 1973 the number of rural seats declined from 181 to 130. Inner-city seats rose for a time from 1962 to 1968 but declined by 1973 to 102. The population increase in the suburbs over this time pushed the number of seats with total or mostly suburban voters to 131, more than any other residential group, thus making them potentially the most powerful bloc in Congress.

However, this statistical factor does not necessarily mean more power in Congress or a greater impact upon legislative politics. Indeed, a Congressional Quarterly voting study done in 1973 indicates that the potential suburban power in Congress had not been realized by that time. Many reasons contribute to the relative powerlessness of the suburban bloc. Leadership posts in Congress usually go to well-recognized and tested members; committee chairmanships were even more narrowly limited to the most senior members of the majority party up until the Ninety-fourth Congress. Since most of the suburban districts were new and redistricting resulted in risky primary and general election battles, the suburban representatives stood less chance to gain leadership posts and wield that type of influence. The safe rural and small town districts continue to provide most of the congressional leadership in spite of the fact that they are a minority.

Furthermore, most, though not all, suburban representatives are Republicans. That party has been the minority and loyal opposition in Congress throughout the period of suburban growth which does not enhance their exercise of power. Party affiliation does influence the voting patterns of

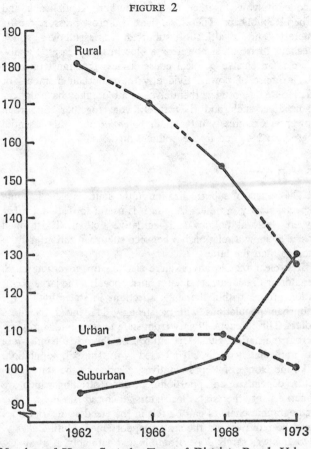

FIGURE 2

Number of House Seats by Type of District: Rural, Urban, Suburban

SOURCES: Richard Lehne, "Shape of the Future," *National Civic Review*, LVIII (Sept. 1969) and Congressional Quarterly, *Weekly Report*, XXXII (April 6, 1974).

representatives. Suburban Democrats and urban Democrats frequently vote together as do suburban Republicans and urban Republicans. Therefore, there is a cross pressure on the interests and loyalties of suburban representatives which weakens their actual power as a bloc in many cases. Finally, there is an elusive political consciousness that must underlie any exercise of power. Evidently the suburban members of the House do not view themselves as a bloc; they have not organized as such and they rarely vote together. Suburban power in Congress must remain *potential* until this essential ingredient is added to the political mix.

THE STATES

The impact of suburbanization in the states is clear in some aspects, cloudy in others. Again, it is useful to distinguish between electoral politics and legislative politics. It is much easier to show a relationship between suburbanization and the former than the latter.

It is clear that in any at-large election for governor, U. S. senator or President, candidates must appeal to the large population groups within the state. Elections in states with large suburban populations will be strongly influenced by those voters. This impact will vary from state to state but is growing across the nation. State legislatures, on the other hand, were not immediately or directly affected by the shifts in population. Like the House of Representatives, election to the state legislature depends upon apportionment and districting which are functions of the state legislators themselves. Before the demographic changes can be felt in the election, district lines must be redrawn and the seats reapportioned. Until *Baker* v. *Carr* this was rarely done promptly and equitably, if at all.

Furthermore, both houses in most state legislatures suffered from similar inequities. It had been assumed by many states that the upper house could reflect interest associated with territoty or region, regardless of population, just as does the U. S. Senate. As population moved a fantastic imbalance in districts occurred.

In 1960 the following conditions prevailed: in Vermont one state representative had a constituency of 24, his colleague had a district of 35,531; in California one senate district had 14,294, another held 6,038,771. In 1966 a Congressional Quarterly publication found "In every house of every state legislature, the largest district was more than twice as large as the smallest district in population terms. The disparity was 424 to 1 in the Connecticut House, 99 to 1 in the Georgia House, 223 to 1 in the Nevada Senate, and 1,414 to 1 in the Rhode Island Senate." Twelve per cent of the people commanded a majority of the Vermont House; 11 per cent controlled a majority in the California Senate. Before reapportionment only 15 per cent of the voters of New Jersey elected the senate majority. Among the most underrepresented in the state legislatures were the new suburbanites who were fast becoming a majority.

Judicial decisions changed this situation dramatically. *Baker* v. *Carr* was actually concerned with the issue of legislative reapportionment in the Tennessee legislature. The judgment, however, opened the federal courts to other plaintiffs suffering the inequalities of dated apportionment plans. The revolution went even further when, on June 15, 1964, the Supreme Court handed down several cases referred to collectively as *Reynolds* v. *Sims*. These decisions destroyed old political customs and challenged the values of the apportionment plans of most states. A key point was that population was to be the basis of apportionment in *both* houses of state legislatures: "Legislators represent people, not trees or acres." The analogy to the U. S. Senate was rejected since the senate plan was frozen into the U. S. Constitution as a result of political compromises in 1787.

As with reapportionment in Congress, by the time it came about in the state legislatures, suburbs, not cities, derived the most benefit from the process. Within two years and in time for the 1966–67 state elections, forty-six states had reapportioned with districts based substantially on population. Continuing litigation brought new reapportionment plans into effect in several states over the following decade. The 1970 census, moreover, created another wave of reapportionments favoring the suburbs in most states.

As William Boyd of the National Municipal League pointed out, "The suburbs and, in the long run, only the suburbs will gain in the upheaval resulting from reapportionment of state legislatures on the basis of population. . . . The suburbs own the future." Typical of these changes is New Jersey which for decades based representation in the senate on the county: one Senator from each regardless of population. Rural Cape May County and urban Essex County, the locus of Newark, had the same representation. When reapportionment took place Cape May was linked to equally rural Cumberland County for apportionment purposes and they share one Senator thereby reducing their representation. Urban and increasingly suburban Essex County has five Senators and Bergen County, dominantly suburban, has five. Overall, the urban and suburban Senators outnumber the rural Senators with the suburban portion surpassing either of the others. This pattern was repeated throughout the country.

Another result of the suburbanization-reapportionment combination was a change in elected personnel and a change in type of personnel. Younger, more urban and suburban and more minority group members have supplanted the rural, aged, and overwhelmingly white legislators of years ago thereby challenging the leadership structures of the legislatures. In some two-party states, like New Jersey, it is expected that with seats being equitably distributed throughout the population, the governor and the legislative majority stand a greater chance of being of the same party. Malapportionment had frequently distorted the political party percentages resulting in a guaranteed majority in either, or both, houses of the legislature for one party while the popular vote for governor was determined by the actual choice of the majority.

Finally, it must be pointed out, most of these changes have already occurred. State legislatures have generally been successfully reapportioned either through court-arranged plans or with the threat of court action in the background. The suburban areas now control their share of votes in virtually every state. The symbol of this success is that after only a decade the Supreme Court is beginning to narrow its action and interest in the area. In *White, Secretary of State of Texas* v. *Regester* (1973) the majority, in overturning a district court decision, said that they should not get "bogged down" in apportionment cases with "minor deviations." Unlike the precedent-setting cases regarding race relations in America, the reapportionment revolution has been successful, and accomplished with a minimum of difficulty.

This analysis demonstrates the impact of suburbanization on the electoral process and on the composition of state legislatures. It leaves the question of the impact on policy outputs of such reapportioned legislatures. This will be considered below. It also leaves the question of the impact of suburbanization on political party affiliation and strength to which we now turn our attention.

POLITICAL PARTY AFFILIATION AND STRENGTH

It has long been part of the folk wisdom of our country that the suburbs are Republican. They vote for Republican candidates for President, Congress, and state office, so the myth goes. The interesting thing is that to a great, but qualified, extent they have but not necessarily always or forever. Another part of the suburban political myth is that as people move "up" to suburbia they move "up" to respectable Republicanism; or that only Republicans move to the suburbs. They don't.

Finally, another consideration is that suburbanization offers the greatest chance to the Republican party to continue as one half of the two-party system. Without the suburbs, the argument goes, the Republican party, already a minority party, would cease to function. Perhaps. Each of these positions will be examined in turn so that we can better understand the impact of suburbanization on political party strength.

The basic question to be answered is, "How Republican are the suburbs?" Evidence can be sought in presidential, congressional, and state and local elections. Each type of election offers a somewhat different picture.

As Figure 3 shows, in all but one postwar presidential election, the Republicans won a majority of suburban votes. The exception was the Goldwater debacle of 1964 when Republican ranks throughout the country broke due to the divisiveness of a noncentrist candidate. While these figures do not distinguish between types of suburbs, there can be no mistake about the long-term, gross pattern: Republican presidential candidates fare well in the suburbs.

FIGURE 3

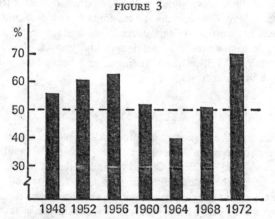

Republican Percentage of Suburban Presidential Vote
SOURCE: Adapted from Lee W. Huebner, "The Republican Party: 1952–1972," *History of U. S. Political Parties,* ed. by Arthur M. Schlesinger (New York, 1973), p. 2987 and the New York *Times,* Dec. 5, 1972.

Congressional election patterns differ only slightly. Frederick Wirt studied the degree to which major suburbs voted Republican in elections from 1932 to 1960 including elections to Congress. As Figure 4 shows, the suburbs voted Republican in all but two of these years. In 1954 and 1958, off-year elections, the Republicans lost ground throughout the country as well as in the suburbs. In 1958 and 1960 they lost the aggregate majority that they had commanded for several years; but Republican dominance in suburban elections returned later in the 1960s with the exception of 1964. As in the 1964 presidential election, the Goldwater candidacy led to a Democratic landslide in all types of districts throughout the country.

FIGURE 4

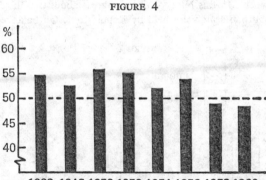

1932 1948 1950 1952 1954 1956 1958 1960

Mean GOP Vote Percentage for Congress in Selected Suburbs
SOURCE: Adapted from F. M. Wirt, "Political Sociology of American Suburbia: A Reinterpretation," *The Journal of Politics,* XXVII (1965), Table 2.

The margins of Republican congressional victories in the suburbs during these years were never so wide as to preclude a reasonable challenge, however. Indeed, as Figure 5 shows, there were always a number of safe Democratic suburbs, although Republicans clearly had the edge in this category. But the suburbs continued to be an arena for two-party politics.

Two notable elections of the 1970s reveal a tenuous balance between the major parties. The congressional election of 1972 was the first based on the new census with its reapportionment and redistricting fallout. Just as in the 1960s, newly created districts benefited the Republicans more than the

Democrats. Seventeen of twenty-four seats that fell to the Republicans did so because of redistricting and reapportionment. Only eight of the fourteen new Democratic seats could be similarly accounted for. Most of these new seats were in the fast-growing suburbs. A complicating factor that seemed to limit even greater Republican gains in 1972 was the fact that Democrats in 1970 had done well in winning state legislatures thereby facilitating Democratic gerrymanders based on the new census. In this Ninety-third Congress about two thirds of the suburban seats were held by Republicans. On balance the

FIGURE 5

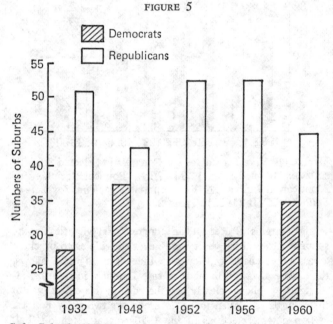

Safe Suburbs for Democrats and Republicans in Congressional Elections
SOURCE: Adapted from F. M. Wirt, "Political Sociology of American Suburbia: A Reinterpretation," *The Journal of Politics,* XXVII (1965), Table 3.

suburbs remained more heavily Republican than Democratic.

On the other hand, 1974 was a year like 1958 and 1964. National reaction to Watergate brought a so-called "veto-proof" Congress to the Republican President. Entrenched Republicans fell all over the country: the Midwest bastion, the new-South, and the suburbs. In that year, of the forty-nine Democratic seats gained, twenty-one were from districts with a majority suburban population. Eight more were from districts with between 40 and 50 per cent suburban population. There were very few Democrat-proof suburbs.

In sum, we find that during most of the years of recent suburban growth, suburbanites were more likely to send Republican Congressmen to Washington, although there were several exceptional years. The margin of the Republican majority was often slim and when the social and economic variety of suburbs are taken into consideration we will see an emerging pattern that challenges the image of solidly Republican suburbs. Short-term factors such as the impact of scandals on a particular election also make it difficult to detect trends. Furthermore, there is a general but firm connection between national electoral trends and suburban trends. More on that below.

When we study state and local electoral patterns the trends are even less distinct. There are many unique features affecting the outcome of these elections, from nonpartisanship to distinctive regional patterns. In the aforementioned study by Wirt the partisan patterns of local elections were analyzed. It is evident that in comparing safe Republican suburban mayoralties with safe Democratic suburban mayoralties, the Republicans are clearly ahead (see Figure 6). However, both types of safe mayoralties declined steadily from the early 1950s while marginal districts (two party and unsafe for either party) increased. It could be that the elusive "good government" ideal of nonpartisanship has taken root most firmly in local suburban elections thereby eroding the significance of party label for both parties along with their political hegemony in many areas. We also can conclude that Republican strength in local politics has waned but that there

FIGURE 6

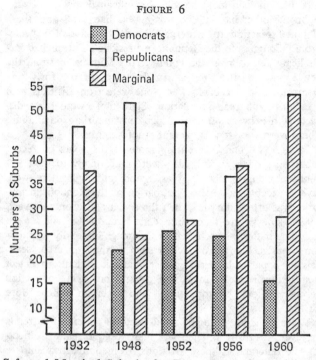

Safe and Marginal Suburbs for Democrats and Republicans in Mayoral Elections

SOURCE: Adapted from F. M. Wirt, "Political Sociology of American Suburbia: A Reinterpretation," *The Journal of Politics*, XXVII (1965), Table 3.

are not enough Democratic voters to claim these districts for their side. In either case the chances are that both parties will continue to battle over local suburban political office; but available evidence indicates a weak Republican dominance with many contested areas.

When studying the effect of suburbanization on state-level partisan trends we find it inextricably bound up with national electoral trends. The first elections for some newly reapportioned state legislatures came during the 1964 Democratic Johnson landslide. For many states this sweep meant that Democrats were in a position to draw up the districting plans for future state elections. We have seen that a similar phenomenon did have an effect on congressional elections in 1972. State issues can also affect partisanship in the suburbs. In the 1965 elections to the state legislatures of two neighboring northern states, New York and New Jersey, almost opposite patterns occurred. In New Jersey a Democratic sweep of normally Republican suburbs gave control of both houses of the state legislature to the Democrats for the first time in fifty years. In the New York legislative race Republicans captured all of the major reapportioned suburban Senate seats and nineteen of twenty-five key suburban Assembly seats. There is little evidence that would lead us to generalize to a national pattern in this area. One regional pattern seems to have appeared, however. In the South the metropolitan growth areas offer the Republican party the greatest chance of growth. This has not yet made them a majority party in the state legislatures, however.

Throughout our discussion we have referred to suburbs in general and have used aggregate data to find the impact of suburban growth on political partisanship. This method has its merits since it is clear that, throughout most of the time studied, Republicans have fared better than Democrats in most elections. But this method does not take into consideration the increasing social and economic variety of suburbs and its impact on partisanship. When suburbs are compared for social and economic factors, patterns appear that can be very useful for predicting future partisan trends.

In Wirt's 1965 study he was testing two theories. One argued the suburbs were becoming more Republican because former Democrats "converted" to Republicanism when they moved "up" to the suburbs. The other was a "transplantation" theory which argued that it was primarily lifelong Republicans that moved to suburbia, thereby accounting for their increased Republican density. The study cast doubt on both of these theories. Instead a diverse pattern emerged of widely varied suburbs: from the wealthy, upper-middle-class type which usually voted Republican to working-class suburbs which usually vote Democratic. Wirt's later study, done with Benjamin Walter, confirms this pattern. The suburbs have continued to diversify and political affiliation, as always, has a high correlation with social and economic factors.

We can conclude that over the years Republicans have dominated suburban politics in key races. In most presidential and congressional elections their leadership is clear but rarely unchallenged. Democrats have always controlled some suburbs and as economic and social diversity increase they have and will continue to successfully challenge established patterns. But the Republican party in suburbia is healthy and is not ceding its votes and seats to the Democrats without a struggle. In state and local elections there are too many complicating and conflicting patterns to establish a clear national trend but it is evident that the suburbs will be the primary arena within which the major parties struggle for political prizes.

POLICY OUTPUTS

Much of what we have studied so far points toward a potentially significant suburban impact upon American politics and government. This potential can be seen in size of suburban delegations in Congress and state legislatures, size of the vote for President and in partisan relationships. However, a fundamental question remains. Has the contemporary suburban phenomenon changed political policy? Several studies have approached this question and there is basic agreement in all of them: malapportionment and/or reapportionment have little or no measurable impact upon recent policy output. However much this flies in the face of American democratic folk wisdom there seems to be little relationship between these phenomena, at least in so far as contemporary modes of analysis can detect.

There was evidence of this in the 1965 study by Thomas R. Dye who compared the policy outputs of well apportioned and malapportioned states. "On the whole," he concluded, "the policy choices of malapportioned legislatures are not noticeably different from the policy choices of well-apportioned legislatures." The next year Richard I. Hofferbert studied the impact of malapportionment on the liberality of state welfare policies and on urban aid patterns. He, too, was unable to find a significant relationship between the variables. The Walter and Wirt study referred to above similarly concluded that constituency cannot account for the voting patterns and policy outputs of representatives. We also have seen that suburban Congressmen do not see themselves in terms that cause them to act in concert in attempting to affect legislative policy. Finally, a 1973 study by Robert E. Firestine confirms these conclusions. In studying the effect of reapportionment upon local government aid receipts he found barely detectable evidence, which is not statistically significant, that reapportionment has changed aid patterns to local government. Together, they might lead to the improbable conclusion that government policy is impervious to wide sweeping changes; but that conclusion is unwarranted. Instead we must rely upon other possible explanations.

It has long been recognized that voting patterns are affected by party affiliation. As we saw with the Congress and as seems to be true elsewhere, Democrats, regardless of constituency and territory, vote most often with Democrats and Republicans with Republicans. Therefore, the reapportionment impact itself might be overshadowed by partisan voting patterns and is immeasurable. Structural factors, such as seniority and leadership customs, might be keeping newer and suburban legislators from having a measurable impact on policy but that seems an explanation limited to only a few legislatures. It might be that the changes in policy actually have occurred but are simply not measurable given the state of the data. Astute observers have reported that reapportionment has made a difference in particular legislatures. In this case it is perhaps only through state-by-state *case studies* that the impact of recent suburbanization upon policy output can be known. So far sophisticated behavioral techniques have not revealed a significant suburban impact on policy.

Part of the answer probably lies in the fact that suburbs had achieved most of their important goals prior to reapportionment and were relatively content with the treatment they were receiving from the federal government and most state legislatures. Hence increased representation for suburbia only meant a continuation of existing policies. The historical dimensions of governmental policies are covered in other essays of this book. However, one only has to recall that federal projects such as the FHA mortgage program and the interstate highway program predated reapportionment and greatly favored the suburbs. State legislation, much of which dates back to the turn of the century, virtually freed suburbs from their dependence on central cities. This was especially true in states such as Massachusetts, New York, and New Jersey.

CRITICAL POLICY CONCERNS

In recent years attention has been focused on two critical policy issues—financial-aid formulae and race relations. In the first case, state financial-aid formulae have traditionally favored rural and more recently suburban areas over cities. For instance, Figure 7 shows the vast discrepancies between cities and suburbs in New York State where ratios in basic areas varied from 16.2 to 1 for certain health programs to 2.1 to 1 for education: the suburbs receiving the lion's share.

The state-supported policy of home rule has allowed American suburbs to try and build barriers against unwanted change. Zoning ordinances, building codes, and tax laws are some of the traditional tools which were employed. These policies compounded the racial problem in this country to the point where the President's Commission on Civil Disorders in 1968 envisioned a specter of black cities surrounded by white suburbs.

The black population had become increasingly urban during recent decades of suburban growth. From 1960 to 1970

FIGURE 7

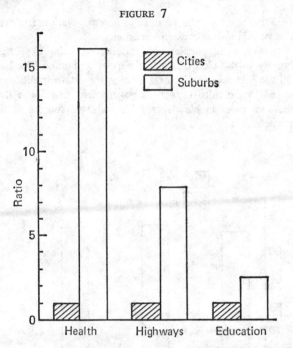

Ratio of State Aid Payments to Suburbs and Cities on a Per Capita Basis for Selected Functions in New York State: 1966–67
SOURCE: Dr. R. B. Pettengill, et al., *Cities and Suburbs: The Case for Equity,* Part 1. (Albany, N.Y.: New York Conference of Mayors and Municipal Officials, 1970), p. 1.

the percentage of the black population living in central cities increased from 44 per cent to 58 per cent. During the same time the percentage of the white population living in the cities decreased from 35 per cent to 27.8 per cent. As Figure 8 indicates, suburbs continued to be overwhelmingly white despite the fact that many blacks began to move to suburbia. Although the black population in suburbia went up by 26.6 per cent between 1960 and 1970 that still left the blacks with only 5 per cent of the total suburban population since the white population also was increasing.

However, these policies and patterns are being challenged primarily in the Courts. Since the poor and minorities have had little influence in electoral politics, they have traditionally resorted to the third branch of government to achieve their ends. Two cases in New Jersey illustrate the success of this approach.

FIGURE 8

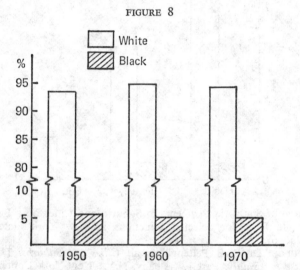

Racial Composition of American Suburbs
SOURCE: U. S. Bureau of the Census, *Statistical Abstract of the U.S.*, p. 16.

In *Southern Burlington County NAACP* v. *Township of Mount Laurel* (New Jersey Superior Court, May, 1972) upheld by the New Jersey Supreme Court March 23, 1975, a town zoning ordinance excluding multifamily housing was declared unconstitutional. It was seen as discriminatory against the poor and minorities who could not afford expensive single-family dwellings. Another case known as the Botter decision has broken the link between local real estate values and educational funding thereby opening the purse strings of affluent suburban communities to the less wealthy urban and rural school districts. Similar decisions have been rendered in California and elsewhere.

Other challenges have been made against suburban privilege primarily in the areas of educational integration and busing. The suburban school patterns of Richmond and Detroit were reviewed by the U. S. Supreme Court and upheld for the time being, but undoubtedly this field will be under constant judicial challenge in order to break allegedly discriminatory suburban patterns.

Conclusion

Recent suburbanization has influenced American government and politics. It has been felt most clearly in electoral politics and in presidential races. The concrete impact it has had upon contemporary legislative politics and policy output is still unclear.

I have tried to point out that the greatest factor in recent suburbanization is its *potential* power for change which still remains dormant. Population shifts and reapportionment have given suburban representatives a numerical advantage in Congress and many state legislatures. Presidential politics already has been influenced by these trends. However, these statistical advantages have been diluted by party affiliation and lack of a national suburban political consciousness. Political scientists disagree why this power has not translated itself into more concrete policy outputs. One possible explanation is that suburbanites have been relatively content with existing government policies and therefore do not feel the need to institute changes.

The most vigorous challenge to suburban privileges ironically have come from the courts which had strengthened suburban political power through reapportionment. If judicially mandated change continues and is dramatic enough, we may well see the potential of suburban political power ac-

tualized through the heightened consciousness of a *status quo*
threatened and a crystallization of voting blocs in Congress
and the several state legislatures.

BIBLIOGRAPHY

THE LITERATURE on contemporary politics and government
in suburbia is generally scattered among works of a more
general nature such as metropolitan and urban political studies, voting analyses, political party surveys, presidential campaign histories, and sociological treatises. Each of these
sources casts some light on the subject, however, and are important to the total picture. A few studies deal directly and
exclusively with suburban political phenomena.

Among the best focused and most fruitful studies are those
of Frederick M. Wirt and his associates. The main concern of
these works was to reveal the diversity and change of suburbia and its politics, thereby challenging the myth of a solid,
upper-class, Republican electorate with clear and well-ar-
ticulated interests. These studies include the articles, "The Political Sociology of American Suburbia: A Reinterpretation,"
The Journal of Politics, XXVII (1965), 647–66 and another jointly authored with Benjamin Walter, "The Political
Consequences of Suburban Variety," *Social Science Quarterly*, LII (Dec. 1971), 746. A book-length study followed
in joint authorship with Walter, F. Rabinowitz, and D.
Hensler, *On the City's Rim: Politics and Policy in Suburbia*
(Lexington, Mass., 1972).

The diversity of suburbia can readily be perceived in the
older work of Bennett M. Berger, *Working-Class Suburb: A
Study of Auto Workers in Suburbia* (Berkeley, 1960) and
the more recent book by George S. Sternlieb, et al., *The Affluent Suburb: Princeton* (New Brunswick, N.J., 1971). Read
together they reveal the wide range of life-style contributing
to diverse political perceptions in suburbia. Two recent anthologies contribute to this theme: John Kramer, ed., *North American Suburbs: Politics, Diversity and Change* (Berkeley, 1972)

and Charles M. Haar, ed., *The End of Innocence* (Glenview, Ill., 1972).

An earlier generation of studies includes the outstanding works of Robert Wood, *Suburbia: Its People and Their Politics* (Boston, 1958) and *1400 Governments* (Cambridge, 1961) wherein he analyzes the complexity and difficulty of self-government in small, autonomous units. The scope and style of government in metropolitan America was a product of conflicting needs and values. Herbert Gans also studied the impact of the suburban life-style on political style in his "Urbanism and Suburbanism as a Way of Life" in *People and Plans: Essays on Urban Problems and Solutions* (New York, 1968) and *The Levittowners: Ways of Life and Politics in a New Suburban Community* (New York, 1967).

As for the specific relevance of suburbia on presidential electoral politics one must see the works on particular campaigns. Among these are the partisan, but useful, tracts of Kevin Phillips, *The Emerging Republican Majority* (New Rochelle, N.Y., 1969) and Richard M. Scammon and Ben J. Wattenberg, *The Real Majority* (New York, 1970). Each gives its own analysis of the political salience of the suburbs to the major parties. A less partisan estimate can be gleaned from Theodore White's series of books, *The Making of the President* (1960–72) and James A. Reichley's article, "As Go the Suburbs, So Goes U.S. Politics," *Fortune*, LXXXII (September, 1970), 105–9, 155–56. See also Joseph Zikmund II, "Suburban Voting in Presidential Elections: 1948–64," *Midwest Journal of Political Science*, XII (May, 1968), 238–56.

The relationships between the suburbs and congressional politics are best analyzed in the various research publications of the Congressional Quarterly service of Washington which include their *Weekly Reports*, the semiannual *Guide to Current American Government* as well as occasional background reports such as *Representation and Apportionment* (Washington, D.C., 1966). These timely and succinct analyses range over the entire field of congressional politics including election returns, reapportionment patterns, voting patterns, and interest articulation.

While some of the above sources can be helpful in understanding the impact of suburbia on state legislative politics, there are a few key articles and other sources worth looking at. Two articles raise serious questions about the long anticipated and somewhat anticlimactic impact of reapportionment upon state legislatures. They are Thomas R. Dye, "Malapportionment and Public Policy in the States," *Journal of Politics,* XXVII (August, 1965), 586–601, and Richard I. Hofferbert, "The Relation Between Public Policy and Some Structural Environmental Variables in the American States," *American Political Science Review,* LX (March, 1966), 73–82. The biannual *Book of the States* publishes up-to-date surveys of state legislatures that are concerned, in part, with the suburban impact. An example is Karl T. Kurtz, "The State Legislatures," *The Book of the States 1974–75,* Volume XX (Lexington, Ky., 1974), 55.

In addition, a limited number of individual state studies have been done giving some data and tentative conclusions in this area such as League of Women Voters of New Jersey, *New Jersey: Spotlight on Government* (New Brunswick, N.J., 1972).

The scope of metropolitan problems is wide and the viewpoints regarding resource distribution, open housing, race, and others are divergent and sometimes hostile. Many attempts have been made to diagnose and prescribe for these regions. Two of these studies point out some of the aspects that divide cities from suburbs: Robert E. Firestine, "The Impact of Reapportionment Upon Local Government Aid Receipts Within Large Metropolitan Areas," *Social Science Quarterly,* LIV (Spring, 1973), 394–402 and Donna E. Shalala, "State Aid to Local Government," *Academy of Political Science Proceedings,* XXXI (May, 1974), 100. Each deals with the basic problem of resource-allocation competition.

Other metropolitan concerns have been treated in many works, especially John C. Bollens and Henry J. Schmandt,

The Metropolis, 2nd. ed. (New York, 1970). On a continuing basis see the *Municipal Year Book,* in particular, Norman Beckman, "Metropolitan Area Trends and Developments," *Municipal Year Book 1974* (Washington, D.C., 1974), 16.

Further research in the field should begin with the excellent bibliography by Louis H. Masotti and Jeffrey K. Hadden, *Suburbs, Suburbia and Suburbanization: A Bibliography* (Monticello, Ill., 1972) published by the Council of Planning Librarians (#269).

THE EFFECT OF SUBURBANIZATION ON THE CITIES
by Kenneth T. Jackson

BY ALMOST ANY STANDARD, Newark is America's sickest city. Its 390,000 residents suffer from the greatest percentage of slum housing, the heaviest property tax burden, and the worst incidence of venereal disease and infant mortality of any large city in the nation. With more than one resident in five receiving some form of public financial assistance, Newark also has the highest percentage of welfare recipients. Stripped automobiles rust in front of abandoned houses and buildings; even the brick sewers are rotting.

Population change has been so rapid in Newark that it will soon become the nation's first virtually all-black city. Gleaming office towers attract an estimated 300,000 workers to the central business district (CBD) every day, but the predominately white commuters have abandoned Newark for the nearby suburbs. Their homes, but not their jobs, have been inherited by almost 150,000 blacks who have migrated to the city since 1950. Some of the newcomers have found employment in New York City, which lies ten miles and twenty minutes to the east; others have joined Newark's declining industries or its busy insurance offices. But in 1976 more than 30 per cent of black males in Newark between the ages of sixteen and twenty-five were unemployed. Not surprisingly, heroin drops along Springfield Avenue are known even to children, and the rate of narcotics addiction is among the highest in the United States.

Not only do social ills plague the body politic, but financial burdens also weaken the community's stability. Newark's small tax base has necessitated a high property tax; in 1974, it was $9.19 per $100 of assessed valuation, triple what it was at the end of World War II. And as an increasing number of property owners have left the city—often because of the confiscatory property tax—the total value of land in the city has actually declined over the last thirty years, forcing the tax rate up still higher. More than 60 per cent of Newark's meager twenty-four square miles is tax exempt, occupied by such facilities as Newark Airport, Port Newark, and the New Jersey College of Medicine and Dentistry.

The myriad difficulties of the New Jersey metropolis have led many to believe that it is a "dying city." But Newark is only an exaggerated example of a malaise that affects dozens of American cities. Core areas throughout the nation house a greater proportion of the poor, the aged, the infirm, and the inadequately educated than the suburbs; at the same time the inner cities lack the resources to deal effectively with such manifestations of social pathology. As Mayor Kenneth Gibson has observed: "Wherever urban America is going, Newark will get there first."

The purpose of this essay is to explore the ways in which suburbanization has contributed to the difficulties of large cities in the United States. In particular, I am concerned with the weakened "sense of community" in metropolitan America, by which I mean the reduced degree of concern and responsibility which suburbanites feel for the plight of core areas. "Community" implies co-operation; if the "sense of community" in metropolitan Newark were strong, then most residents of bucolic Scotch Plains, Glen Ridge, Short Hills, and other suburbs would have a clear and positive identification with the larger metropolis. They would believe that they are united in a way that other citizens of New Jersey are not.

Citizen identification with the city is less now than it was a century and more ago. To be sure, nineteenth-century communities were bothered by crime, class rigidity, social unrest, epidemics, and disastrous fires. But they possessed a significant sense of local pride and spirit as a result of their struggles with other cities for canals, railroads, factories, and state institutions. In our own time, most observers have noted that alienation and anomie are more characteristic of urban life than a sense of participation and belonging.

In my view there are four reasons why this unfortunate circumstance has come about: (1) the residential polarization of urban neighborhoods and suburbs by income and race, (2) the failure of municipalities to extend their boundaries through annexation and consolidation, (3) the widespread adoption of the private automobile as the primary means of urban transportation, and (4) the changing nature of modern entertainment. All are closely bound up with what one might call suburbanization or the suburban way of life.

THE RESIDENTIAL POLARIZATION OF THE METROPOLIS

If we take suburbanization to mean that people move away from the center city in a search for living space, then suburbanization is an old process in the United States, dating back until at least 1820, when bucolic Brooklyn was growing at Manhattan's expense. Before about 1850, however, commercial and residential districts had been ill-defined and overlapping, and the rich and the poor had often lived in close proximity. Despite the availability of inexpensive land on the urban periphery, city inhabitants crowded closely together. Because the most common method of getting about was by foot, there was a significant advantage in living within easy walking distance of the city's stores and businesses. Not surprisingly, the most fashionable and respectable residential addresses were close to the center of town.

Between 1850 and 1930, however, America's large cities underwent a startling spatial transformation characterized by the exodus of the middle and upper classes. The shift was not sudden, but it was no less profound for its gradual character.

By the 1920s, sociologists at the University of Chicago had constructed a concentric zone model to describe the way in which residential neighborhoods improved in quality with increasing distance from the core. This "North American pattern" became so dominant that a suburban rabbi recently confessed that when he was growing up in Brooklyn, the posh Five Towns area of Long Island, even more than Israel, represented the "promised land."

Newark offers a good example of this trend. In the nineteenth century, the New Jersey metropolis was one of the nation's leading industrial centers. Its heavy industries, its whirring factories, its prosperous building trades, and its noted public works made it a confident and optimistic community. As late as 1927, a prominent Newark businessman boasted:

> Great is Newark's vitality. It is the red blood in its veins—this basic strength that is going to carry it over whatever hurdles it may encounter, enable it to recover from whatever losses it may suffer and battle its way to still higher achievement industrially and financially, making it eventually perhaps the greatest industrial center in the world.

Yet the suburban migration was already draining away Newark's most successful and prosperous citizens. By 1925, more than 40 per cent of the attorneys whose offices were in Newark were themselves living in the suburbs; by 1947 the figure had jumped to 63 per cent, and by 1965 to 78 per cent. Members of the city's leading booster association abandoned their home community in even greater numbers. In 1932, more than 86 per cent of the officers and board of directors of the Newark Chamber of Commerce lived in the suburbs.

Patterns in other cities were less startling but similar. In staid Boston, more than half of the Hub's lawyers were living outside the city as early as 1911; by 1971, three out of four were sleeping in the suburbs. In New York City, considerable prestige has always accrued to attorneys who work in the towering office skyscrapers of Manhattan, where they can operate in the reflected glow of the world's corporate, financial, and communications nerve center. Moreover, the "Big Apple" offers, in Greenwich Village and the Upper East Side, glamorous residential areas that are convenient to such symbols of power and wealth as priceless museums, chauffeured limousines, five-star restaurants, glittering entertainment, and ultraselective clubs. Yet, about two-thirds of all lawyers practicing in Manhattan in 1973 commuted in the evening to the suburbs in Westchester County, Long Island, or New Jersey.

It was not inevitable, in Newark or Boston or New York or anywhere else, that the middle and upper classes would gravitate to the urban edges. But actions of the government, at the local level through zoning, and at the national level through long-term mortgage loans, helped to insure that metropolitan areas would be segregated by income and race. The result has been as detrimental to cities as it has been beneficial to most suburbs. The core, as everyone now well knows, has become identified with poor people, blacks, deterioration, older dwellings, and abandoned buildings. Middle- and upper-income suburbs convey the opposite impression.

This racial and economic polarization is a major reason why fear has become such a common emotion in our metropolitan areas. In Memphis, the homicide rate, although deplorably high, is less than half what it was in 1915, when the Bluff City was regionally notorious as a "murder capital." Yet Memphis' downtown was bustling and vibrant in 1915; in 1976, it is dormant to such a degree that one could fire a 155 mm. howitzer down Main Street at eight o'clock in the evening without much chance of creating a casualty. In Newark, the streets are also dark and deserted, and a businessman there recently complained: "Since the riots, many people—both black and white—have been afraid to come to Newark at night. We've lost many customers."

It might be noted that this fear has little relation to reality; that blacks are more likely to be robbed, raped, or murdered than whites; that the suburbs are increasingly the scene of the same kind of mayhem that their inhabitants fled the city to escape; that Newark actually has a relatively low incidence of major crime. Yet this is an instance in which the image is as important as reality. For example, New York is a city which

TABLE 1

RATE OF VIOLENT CRIME PER 1,000 RESIDENTS AGE 12 AND OVER IN THIRTEEN SELECTED AMERICAN CITIES, 1972

	Ratio of Unreported to Reported Crime	Rape	Robbery	Assault	Total Crimes of Violence
DETROIT	2.7 to 1	3	32	33	68
DENVER	2.9 to 1	3	17	46	67
PHILADELPHIA	5.1 to 1	1	28	34	63
PORTLAND	2.6 to 1	3	17	40	59
CHICAGO	2.8 to 1	3	26	27	56
BALTIMORE	2.2 to 1	1	26	28	55
CLEVELAND	2.4 to 1	2	24	28	54
LOS ANGELES	2.9 to 1	2	16	35	53
ATLANTA	2.3 to 1	2	16	30	48
DALLAS	2.6 to 1	2	10	31	43
NEWARK	1.4 to 1	1	29	12	42
ST. LOUIS	1.5 to 1	1	16	25	42
NEW YORK CITY	2.1 to 1	1	24	11	36

The ratios are based on a sample of 22,000 residents and 2,000 businessmen in each city and a standard set of questions.
SOURCE: National Crime Panel Surveys, Law Enforcement Assistance Administration, United States Department of Justice.

TABLE 2

RATE OF NON-VIOLENT HOUSEHOLD
VICTIMIZATION PER 1,000 HOUSEHOLDS IN
THIRTEEN SELECTED AMERICAN CITIES, 1972

	Burglary	Household Larceny	Auto Theft	Total Non-Violent Crimes
DENVER	158	168	44	370
PORTLAND	151	149	34	334
DETROIT	174	106	49	329
LOS ANGELES	148	131	42	321
DALLAS	147	147	24	318
ATLANTA	161	102	29	292
CLEVELAND	124	80	76	280
ST. LOUIS	125	81	47	253
BALTIMORE	116	100	35	251
PHILADELPHIA	109	87	42	238
CHICAGO	118	77	36	231
NEWARK	123	44	37	204
NEW YORK CITY	68	33	26	127

Information for the five largest cities (New York, Chicago, Los Angeles, Philadelphia, and Detroit) was based on the 1972 calendar year. Information for the eight others is based on surveys carried out in July–October, 1972 covering the previous twelve months.
SOURCE: National Crime Panel Surveys, Law Enforcement Assistance Administration, United States Department of Justice.

fills many people with terror, partly because of its incomparable size and physical concentration and partly because of its reputation for crime. As Tables 1 and 2 indicate, however, an extensive Department of Justice analysis of thirteen major cities recently confirmed what police experts already knew—New York City is rather sedate when compared with other places. Similarly, a subway ride is statistically far safer than any other form of ground transportation, but the popular image of crime obviously keeps some people off the trains. Criminologists suggest that the disparity between the image and the fact may lie in Manhattan's position as the television and publishing center of the world. United Press International and the Associated Press, as well as *Time, Newsweek,* and the nightly network news programs, all originate in New York. Most book publishers are headquartered in Gotham, and both the *Wall Street Journal* and the New York *Times* have an influence and a readership far beyond the limits of city's boundaries. Because editors, writers, and producers are disproportionately located in the metropolitan area, the crime experience of the city may be subtly and repeatedly offered to Americans through reading and viewing.

The Breakdown of Annexation

The second problem of suburbanization has been the failure of cities to extend their boundaries through annexation or consolidation. In the nineteenth century, suburbs lost their separate identity because municipal governments adopted the philosophy that "bigger is better" and expanded their populations and area by moving their boundaries outward. In this way cities were able to recapture citizens who were using horsecars, trolleys, and steam railroads to move to new homes in the suburbs. Without exception, such adjustments have represented the dominant method of population growth in every American city. If annexation or consolidation had not taken place, there now would be no great cities in the United States in the political sense of the term. Only New York City would have grown as large as one million people, and it would have remained confined to the island of Manhattan. Viewed another way, if annexation had not been successful in the nineteenth century, many large cities would have been surrounded by suburbs even before the Civil War.

In some metropolitan regions, the addition of new land to the central city continues to this day. Indianapolis recently became the tenth largest city in the United States by virtue of its absorption of most of Marion County. In Memphis, Jacksonville, Oklahoma City, Houston, Phoenix, and Dallas a similar annexation process has continued. Thus, these cities registered startling population gains between 1960 and 1970; in actuality, what was called growth was the building up and annexation of residential communities on the edges.

This has not been the experience of most of the large, older cities in the United States. Throughout the twentieth century, their outlying neighborhoods and suburbs have increasingly chosen to reject political absorption into the larger metropolis. In St. Louis, Pittsburgh, Cleveland, San Francisco, Philadelphia, and New York, for example, municipal boundaries have not been altered in half a century and the core areas are being strangled by a tight ring of suburbs.

The negative consequences of governmental fragmentation are especially evident in Newark. It is the only major city in the United States which has lost more territory than it has gained, and its minuscule twenty-four-square-mile area is the dominant cause of many of its contemporary problems. Like every other large community, Newark wanted to annex its suburbs. And its leaders confidently expected that New Jersey's largest city would follow the example set by many other metropolitan areas. As the mayor of Newark remarked in 1900: "East Orange, Vailsburg, Harrison, Kearny, and Belleville would be desirable acquisitions. By an exercise of discretion we can enlarge the city from decade to decade without unnecessarily taxing the property within our limits, which has already paid the cost of public improvements."

But Newark was stifled. While nearby suburbs prospered, the city increasingly became the home of poor minorities. Perceptive observers realized by the 1930s that the future was

bleak. In that decade Princeton University economist James
G. Smith noted that Newark had potential "comparable to
the phenomenal growth of Los Angeles." But he predicted
that "Newark must create a hegemony over her lesser neighbors or find her great destiny aborted." But the suburbs
wanted no part of the industrial city and, in 1933, a Newark
commissioner told the local Optimist Club:

> Newark is not like the city of old. The old, quiet residential
> community is a thing of the past, and in its place has come a
> city teeming with activity. With the change has come some-
> thing unfortunate—the large number of outstanding citizens who
> used to live within the community's boundaries has dwindled.
> Many of them have moved to the suburbs and their home in-
> terests are there.

The fact that the peripheral neighborhoods had then and
usually have now the legal status of separate communities has
given them the capacity to zone out the poor, to refuse public
housing, and to resist the integrative forces of the modern
metropolis. Thus, the problems of some neighborhoods, usually located in the core cities, are more serious than those of
adjacent communities, usually suburbs. And because the suburbs are independent and have their own traditions and history, people who grow up in Brookline, or Bronxville, or
Lake Forest, or Arcadia, or East Orange tend to offer their
primary loyalties to their suburb and to deny responsibility
for those who reside a few miles away. In Philadelphia, an
angry letter to the editor recently expressed just such a view:

> It is ridiculous to suppose that those of us in the suburbs have
> any responsibility to help in the current Philadelphia school
> crisis. We did not create the problems of the inner city and we
> are not obligated to aid in their solution.

Resistance to annexation is symptomatic of a general shift
in the meaning of "suburban." Whereas the word once im-
plied a relationship with the city, the term today is more
likely to represent a distinction from the city. The nomenclature of peripheral communities suggests the accuracy of this
proposition. Among the older suburbs of Chicago, for in-

stance, one can find a North Chicago, a West Chicago, an East Chicago, a Chicago Heights, and a South Chicago Heights. More recently, the Windy City's suburbs have adopted names more suggestive of the countryside than the Loop. In that single metropolitan area, twenty-four separate communities have taken either "Park" or "Forest" in their names; other popular terms seem to be "Hills," "Estates," and various forms of "dales." How different from the nineteenth century, when aspiring settlements used to incorporate the word "city" into their very name—Oklahoma City, Virginia City, Dodge City, Carson City, New York City—in the hope that the wish might father the fact. But the best example of the relevance of suburban place names to the decline of metropolitan feeling comes from East Paterson, New Jersey, which in 1973 changed its name to Elmwood Park. The former title designated a close, spatial relationship with a seedy, industrial city; the second is suggestive of a quiet residential setting.

Professional sports nomenclature also offers a clue to the changing "sense of community" in metropolitan America. The designation of a place or a team by a name—a specific name under which fans or residents can unite—is one piece of evidence that a community exists. Until about 1960, athletic teams were almost always known by the names of the central cities they represented: the New York Yankees, the Chicago White Sox, the Boston Celtics, the San Francisco Giants, the Cleveland Indians. In recent years, however, there has been a trend away from naming teams for cities, as if an association with the core city would limit box office appeal. Thus we have the Minnesota Twins, the California Angels, the Texas Rangers, the Golden State Warriors, the Indiana Pacers, the Kentucky Colonels, even the New England Patriots. In the 1950s, the Brooklyn Dodgers attracted fans all over the nation through radio broadcasts of regular games; in the 1970s, it would no longer be possible to name a team after one section of one city.

The Automobile

The third cause of the weakness of community spirit in metropolitan America is the private car and the type of road system it has spawned. Without dwelling on the fact that automobiles are responsible for 50,000 deaths per year in the United States (down about 8,000 since the reduction of speed limits to 55 miles per hour), that they are the principal source of air pollution, that they guzzle millions of barrels of oil every day and hold us hostage to the oil-exporting countries, that they cause traffic jams that shatter our nerves and clog the cities they were supposed to open up, or that they are turning the countryside to pavement, it is relevant to discuss the way the automobile has changed the way of life of city residents and has become the most powerful instrument for changing the urban landscape ever devised.

Consider the problem of the downtown area. Many people wrongly assume that suburbanization is the cause of central business district difficulty. Actually, the suburbs were growing at unprecedented rates between 1880 and 1930, which was clearly the golden age of the downtown. The reason is that while the electric streetcar (and later the motorbus) enabled urban residents to live farther and farther away from the urban center, it did not allow them to break their ties with the core. The streetcar tracks radiated out from the CBD like spokes on a wheel. Lateral or cross-town service on the trolley was usually very poor. If you wanted to go somewhere, you went by mass transit; in 1912, for example, every person who lived in a city of 100,000 or more rode public transportation an average of 252 times per year. And if you went by mass transit, you went downtown. At the junction of these streetcar lines, the crowds were the heaviest and the land values the highest. In 1930, for example, the less than one square mile of the Chicago Loop accounted for more than 40 per cent of the total land value in a city of more than two hundred square miles. Appropriately, the Loop in Chicago is defined by the elevated tracks which circle the downtown central business district.

Among the symbols of the downtown era were the skyscrapers, which easily topped the spires of the old churches and which seemed to indicate that there were new temples in urban America, and the opulent hotels, which, like the Waldorf-Astoria and the Plaza in New York and the Palmer House and the Drake in Chicago, were the centers of lavish private entertainment and of the most important public celebrations.

But more than anything else, the streetcar era coincided with the rise of the great downtown department store. In 1870, there were no such institutions in this country. But in the next half century, huge mercantile emporiums like Macy's, Gimbel's, Bloomingdale's, and Lord and Taylor in New York; Marshall Field and Carson, Pirie, Scott in Chicago; John Wanamaker's in Philadelphia; Jordan Marsh in Boston; Hudson's in Detroit; Stewart's in Louisville; Rike's in Dayton; Rich's in Atlanta; and Goldsmith's in Memphis became practically synonymous with the cities in which they were located.

The automobile changed the urban balance once again and caused the decay of central business districts throughout the country. Certainly, the private car did more than simply add additional layers to the streetcar suburbs which already surrounded every major city. Unlike the fixed streetcar tracks, which almost always led downtown and thus encouraged transit patrons to maintain their social and economic ties to the core, the private car could go almost anywhere there was a road. For a time, increases in motor travel merely meant that it was easier for more people to get to the city for shopping. Soon, however, downtown sections became hopelessly congested, and the ease of moving about was canceled out by the impossibility of finding a place to stop within a reasonable distance from the retail stores. Later, when parking lots and parking garages were opened by the score, unhappy city officials belatedly realized that they had paved over and obliterated the small shops and specialty stores that had given the old downtown a special kind of vitality and excitement.

As the number of internal-combustion vehicles on the road increased and as public transit patronage decreased, it became clear that the automobile was reshaping the physical city. In the New York area, Robert Moses became the greatest builder and most powerful nonelected public official the United States has yet produced by constructing massive highways, bridges, and other public works according to his "rubber tire mentality." When Moses came to power in 1934, New York's mass transit system was the best in the world. When he lost influence in 1968, it was among the worst (although still the busiest and most extensive). In those years more than six hundred miles of controlled access expressways were built in the metropolitan area; not a single mile of subway was initiated. Moses refused even to acquire the space for possible future rail lines, although he could have done so in the median strips of his highways at relatively little cost. And he not only prohibited buses from his parkways, but he built the overpasses so low that buses could never use them. The real tragedy for New York was that the man who guided its twentieth-century development, the man whose opinions outweighed those of anyone else, did not really like the city and did not really have a feel for its neighborhoods and its diversity. Instead, he "was America's, and probably the world's, most vocal, effective, and prestigious apologist for the automobile." According to such a philosophy, trolley tracks were ripped up "to promote the flow of traffic."

Not only in New York, but in every major city in the country, beltways around the built-up area and cross-town or lateral arteries were built, which encouraged the growth of suburbs and spurred the construction of 14,000 shopping centers by 1970 to meet the retail needs of the new peripheral residents. Meanwhile, the Main Streets of America were transformed into collections of dusty, underused shops, parking lots, and blighted warehouses. Venerable old hostelries lost customers, giving into the years, slipping into shoddiness, even permanently locking their revolving doors. In 1973, before the energy crisis, an old hotel was closing every thirty hours somewhere in downtown America. And somewhere in suburban America, a new hotel was opening every thirty hours. In fact, a new word, "motel," was coined to describe the plastic palaces on the beltways.

The road, not the department store, became the symbol of the new suburban culture. The highway strips, with their fast food outlets, flashing neon signs, and tacky automobile showrooms, became the new area of brief informal communication and social interaction. As J. B. Jackson has observed, a drive through any medium-sized city in America after dark will indicate at once that all the vitality is concentrated along the highway—not along Main Street and certainly not along the shady, curvilinear roads of the suburbs. Even church pews may fall victim to the American love affair with the automobile. In suburban Garden Grove, California, a huge community church, situated appropriately on twenty acres of land near a freeway interchange, offers its six thousand communicants the benefits of drive-in religious inspiration. Ushers step up to the car window and direct the driver's attention to the announcement: "If you have a car radio, please turn to 540 on your dial for this service. If you do not have a radio, please park by the amplifiers in the back row."

THE CHANGING NATURE OF MODERN ENTERTAINMENT

The final aspect of suburbanization I would mention as a cause of the weakened "sense of community" in metropolitan America is the changing use of leisure and especially the establishment of the home as a self-sufficient entertainment center. In the nineteenth century, leisure was a precious and rare commodity, and retirement was a little-known concept. But men and women have always had some time of their own, and the use of that time provides a good indication of their attitudes toward community life.

Cities, by their very nature, ought to encourage the elevation of the human spirit. Anyone who has ever visited the Piazza San Marco in Venice, or shared the happy conviviality of Tivoli Gardens in Copenhagen, or marveled at the temptations of the Reeperbahn in Hamburg, or strolled at midnight

along the Ramblas in Barcelona, or gone Sunday bicycling in
Central Park in New York knows something of the potentiali-
ties and varieties of urban experience. They remind one of
Samuel Johnson's telling phrase: "When a man is tired of
London, he is tired of life."

American cities boast of concert halls, opera houses, ballet
companies, museums, and shopping streets as distinguished as
any in the world. But in the United States, as Robert C.
Wood has observed, what is most significant is not the
influence of modern culture, but the general suburban resistance to it. What is striking in the lives of most residents is the
frequency with which they choose not to avail themselves of
the variety of experiences the metropolis affords, the manner
in which they voluntarily restrict their interests and associations to the immediate vicinity, and the way in which they decline contacts with the larger society.

Suburbanites are of course not completely private in their
associations. Occasionally, they join a hunt club, which has
probably never run a fox to ground, or a country club, which
is almost never in the country. In general, however, we focus
our leisure and our energies on the home. Our idea of the
good life is to build a French provincial house with an enormous hand-hewn shingle roof such as was never seen in any
French province. Then we install a patio or a swimming pool
for friendly outdoor living.

The real shift, however, is the way in which our lives are
now centered inside the house, rather than on the street or in
the neighborhood. There are few places as desolate and lonely
as a suburban street on a hot afternoon. A half century and
more ago, a house was a place to get out of. The ventilation,
lighting, and heat were atrocious; it was hot in summer and
cold in winter. Among its few pleasures were reading and
making love. The miracles of modern technology have
changed some of that.

First, with the old crank-up phonograph and crystal sets,
and more recently with the wide availability of stereophonic
music, color television, and air conditioning, the private
dwelling offers a wide range of comforts and possibilities, and

with the expansion of telephone service, easy and quick communication with outsiders. Old neighborhood institutions, once accessible by foot or by streetcar, have crumbled. In Newark, only fourteen of an original sixty-five movie theaters remained in the city in 1972. The once popular Liberty, the Savoy, and the Weequahic have been demolished in massive urban-renewal programs. Television, rising costs, and drive-ins caused the deaths of others such as the 2,540-seat Loew's State opposite Military Park; the Avon Theater, now a vacant store; and the once prosperous Stanley Theater, now a little-used "culture center."

Not only in Newark, but in every American city, many people now regard it as a waste of time and money to go out to a game or to a concert or to a movie, what with the Green Bay Packers and Lawrence Welk available in the family room. Because the action of the individual is passive and private rather than active and communal, Columbia University anthropologist Margaret Mead has referred to such rooms as giant playpens into which the parents have crawled.

CONCLUSION

In summary, various tendencies associated with suburbanization have had a negative impact on the vitality of cities in America. It is not that we no longer have loyalties. In an era of high mobility and instant communication, we probably identify more than ever with national professional associations, with special-interest groups, and perhaps with urban dwellers as a class. And we also retain considerable identity with our immediate neighborhood or suburb. As people move to new subdivisions and create new churches, new schools, and new social organizations, they are after all engaged in community building. But a weakened sense of concern for the city has been the price of suburban pride.

There are those who think the city is doomed and who applaud the tendency of each person to "do his own thing" and be concerned only with his immediate turf. Neighborhood control has a powerful appeal in contemporary America; indeed, in fields such as education, waste collection, and street repair, decentralization of political authority may be the best solution. But each metropolitan area should also be viewed as a whole, or as a living organism, in which problems in one part may as safely be ignored as cancer in an obscure part of the human body. Suburban areas may themselves one day become slums; in 1890, Harlem was a pleasant, bedroom community for lower Manhattan. Suburban legal independence allows them to resist change, but the process of metropolitan growth is a powerful force that will not be denied.

An economic investment in the metropolis is not enough; we must make an intellectual and moral commitment to the city. It is one of the ironies of the twentieth century that in an age of cities, American cities are decaying. While real trolleys in Newark, Philadelphia, Pittsburgh, and Boston languish for lack of patronage and government support, millions of people flock to Disneylands and Six Flags to ride fake trains that don't go anywhere. Our environment is becoming bland and plastic; our world full of McDonald's and Holiday Inns, each one looking exactly like the one before. Suburbs themselves, although parklike and pleasant, usually have as much distinctiveness and character as a shopping center. With a few exceptions, if you have seen one, you have seen them all.

How different it is with the central city and with the metropolis as a whole. There is not an important city anywhere in America that does not have a unique character, a particular spirit, and a fascinating history. Each city has a peculiar location and appearance; unlike the mass-produced suburbs, no intelligent observer could mistake Baltimore for Chicago, Minneapolis for Milwaukee, Los Angeles for Houston, or Portland for Memphis. The old downtown can give metropolitan residents, including suburbanites, a sense of place, a sense of uniqueness, and a sense of belonging.

Suburbs clearly represent the type of environment in which most Americans would like to live. Hemingford and Alliance, small towns in western Nebraska, are appropriate for some people, and Greenwich Village and the Upper West Side in New York are appropriate for a rather different sort of being.

But the majority of this nation's citizens want a detached house, on a generous plot of ground, within easy access of a large city. Such a choice need not mean the death of urban communities as we know them. Rather, it is important for peripheral residents generally and suburban residents in particular to realize that the health and prosperity of urban centers is in the long run a necessary prerequisite for the health and prosperity of the suburbs. When Boeing reduces its work force in Seattle, or General Motors shuts down in Detroit, the economic impact is felt immediately across and through suburban boundaries. The parts cannot thrive independently of the whole; American cities not only are worth saving, but they must be saved. In this regard, I am fond of quoting Charles E. Merriam, a noted political scientist at the University of Chicago in the first third of this century: "The trouble with Lot's wife was that she looked backward and saw Sodom and Gomorrah. If she had looked forward, she would have seen that heaven is also pictured as a city."

BIBLIOGRAPHY

THERE IS NO general study of the effect of suburbanization on the cities. There are, however, a number of inquiries into the current state of urban America. Among the better analyses are Jane Jacobs, *The Death and Life of Great American Cities* (New York, 1961); Edward Banfield, *The Unheavenly City* (Boston, 1971); and Sam Bass Warner, Jr., *The Urban Wilderness: A History of the American City* (New York, 1972), especially parts one and three. The standard work on the emerging urban area that stretches from southern New Hampshire to northern Virginia and centers on New York City is Jean Gottmann, *Megalopolis: The Urbanized Northeastern Seaboard of the United States* (Cambridge, Mass., 1961). The most influential study of contemporary American housing development is Richard F. Muth, *Cities and Housing: The Spatial Pattern of Urban Residential Land Use* (Chicago, 1969).

Harlan Paul Douglass, *The Suburban Trend* (New York, 1925) was the first monograph to focus entirely on the residential periphery. A more recent overview is Kenneth T. Jackson, "The Crabgrass Frontier: 150 Years of Suburban Growth in America," in Raymond Mohl and James F. Richardson, eds., *The Urban Experience* (Belmont, Calif., 1973), pp. 196–221. Other important studies are Charles N. Glaab, "Metropolis and Suburb: The Changing American City," in John Braeman, et al., eds., *Change and Continuity in Twentieth Century America: The 1920's* (Columbus, Ohio, 1968), pp. 399–437; and Joseph L. Arnold, *The New Deal in the Suburbs: A History of the Greenbelt Town Program, 1935–1954* (Columbus, Ohio, 1971).

The classic description of the process of urban growth is E. W. Burgess, "The Growth of the City," in Robert E. Park, E. W. Burgess, and R. D. McKenzie, eds., *The City* (Chicago, 1925), pp. 47–62. Marion Clawson, *Suburban Land Conversion in the United States: An Economic and Governmental Process* (Baltimore, 1971) is long, detailed, and sophisticated. On the history of metropolitan spatial patterns, the best studies are: Joel Tarr, *Transportation Innovation and Changing Spatial Patterns: Pittsburgh, 1850–1910* (Pittsburgh, 1972); David Ward, "The Emergence of Central Immigrant Ghettoes in American Cities, 1840–1920," *Annals, Association of American Geographers*, LVIII (June, 1968), 343–59; Allen Pred, *The Spatial Dynamics of Urban Industrial Growth, 1800–1914: Interpretive and Theoretical Essays* (Cambridge, Mass., 1966); and Kenneth T. Jackson, "Urban Deconcentration in the Nineteenth Century: A Statistical Inquiry," in Leo F. Schnore, ed., *The New Urban History: Quantitative Explorations by American Historians* (Princeton, 1975), pp. 110–42. A study of an English suburb that is more descriptive than analytical is Harold James Dyos, *Victorian Suburb: A Study of the Growth of Camberwell* (Leicester, England, 1961). John Rannells, *The Core of the City* (New York, 1956) is also useful.

The relationship between mass transit and the growth of the urban fringe has been covered in James Leslie Davis, *The*

Elevated System and the Growth of Northern Chicago (Evanston, Ill., 1965); Edwin H. Spengler, *Land Values in New York in Relation to Transit Facilities* (New York, 1930); Harry J. Carman, *The Street Surface Railway Franchises of New York City* (New York, 1919); Glen E. Holt, "The Changing Perception of Urban Pathology: An Essay on the Development of Mass Transit in the United States," in Kenneth T. Jackson and Stanley K. Schultz, eds., *Cities in American History* (New York, 1972), pp. 324–43; and David Ward, "A Comparative Historical Geography of Streetcar Suburbs in Boston, Massachusetts and Leeds, England, 1850–1920," *Annals, Association of American Geographers,* LIV (1964), 477–89. Sam Bass Warner, *Streetcar Suburbs: The Process of Growth in Boston, 1870–1900* (Cambridge, Mass., 1962), is the best single study of the subject. The deconcentration of manufacturing activity is considered in James B. Kenyon, *Industrial Localization and Metropolitan Growth: The Paterson-Passaic District* (Chicago, University of Chicago Department of Geography Research Paper No. 67, 1960).

Most of the literature on the automobile is vapid and antiquarian. Bellamy Partridge, *Fill'er Up: The Story of Fifty Years of Motoring* (New York, 1952), and Floyd Clymer, *Henry's Wonderful Model T: 1908–1927* (New York, 1955), are typical in that they are uncritical books about auto races and the changes in style and color. Even the more scholarly works of John B. Rae, such as *The Road and the Car in American Life* (Cambridge, Mass., 1971), largely praises rather than analyzes that vital industry. The most useful volumes are James J. Flink, *America Adopts the Automobile, 1895–1910* (Cambridge, Mass., 1970); Raymond M. Wik, *Henry Ford and Grassroots America* (Ann Arbor, Mich., 1972); and Allan Nevins and Frank Ernest Hill, *Ford, Expansion and Challenge, 1915–1933,* II (New York, 1957). For a horrifying account of the role of General Motors in the destruction of the nation's streetcar system, see Bradford C. Snell, "American Ground Transport: A Proposal for Restructuring the Automobile, Truck, Bus, and Rail Industries," Presented to the Subcommittee on Antitrust and Monopoly of the Committee on the Judiciary, U. S. Senate, February 26, 1974, 93rd Congress, 2nd Sess.

The most recent overview of the history of annexation is Kenneth T. Jackson, "Metropolitan Government Versus Suburban Autonomy: Politics on the Crabgrass Frontier," in Jackson and Schultz, eds., *Cities in American History*, pp. 442–62. Earlier studies which remain useful are: Richard Bigger and James D. Kitchen, *How the Cities Grew: A Century of Municipal Independence and Expansion in Metropolitan Los Angeles* (Los Angeles: Bureau of Governmental Research, 1952); Thomas Barclay, *The St. Louis Home Rule Charter of 1876* (Columbia, Mo., 1962); Victor Jones, *Metropolitan Government* (Chicago, 1942); Brett W. Hawkins, *Nashville Metro: The Politics of City-County Consolidation* (Nashville, Tenn., 1966); Howard Lee McBain, *The Law and the Practice of Municipal Home Rule* (New York, 1916); and Roderick D. McKenzie, *The Metropolitan Community* (New York, 1933).

The changing use of spare time in Westchester County is considered in George A. Lundberg, et al., *Leisure: A Suburban Study* (New York, 1934). Two of the most provocative and informative studies of houses in the United States are Leonard K. Eaton, *Two Chicago Architects and Their Clients: Frank Lloyd Wright and Howard Van Doren Shaw* (Cambridge, Mass., 1969); and Charles Moore, Gerald Allen, and Donlyn Lyndon, *The Place of Houses* (New York, 1974).

THE ARTS AND THE SUBURBS
by C. G. Vasiliadis

SUBURBAN AMERICA is often envied for many aspects of its life-style, especially when compared to the environment of a large city. Lower crime rates, cleaner air, homogeneous settings, home ownership, and good schools have drawn millions of Americans to this middle landscape. However, the arts were never part of the lure of suburbia. If there is one element in which cities feel clearly superior to their suburban neighbors, it is in the arts. The relative absence of culture in suburbia is one of the major reasons for its stereotyped image of blandness. In fact, for many, suburban culture is simply a contradiction in terms and is therefore dismissed or, worse, not even discussed.

At first glance this attitude seems natural. Cities such as Fort Worth, Minneapolis, Atlanta, Kansas City, St. Louis, Boston, Cleveland, and Chicago dominate the cultural landscape and a viable suburban alternative has not yet appeared in these areas. For example, Chicago maintains a strong dominance over its neighboring suburbs. Its suburban communities are veritable bedrooms of the Loop; whatever cultural life exists beyond city limits is of a neighborhood variety and unassuming proportions. For the Chicago suburbanite, the city is the main cultural resource with little in the way of competition from the surrounding communities. It is interesting to note that there are few, if any, professionally administered arts councils in the Chicago suburbs, thus making a study of local arts activities a virtual impossibility.

Yet on the outskirts of New York, San Francisco, Washington, D.C., and some other large cities, the arts are taking root and growing. Admittedly, this development is relatively new and the topic itself defies simple classification since the relationship between suburban communities and the arts are as varied as the arts themselves. Further it must be said that the suburbs most heavily involved in the arts are among the most affluent in the country. It is a fact of life, and by no means unique to this age, that the arts flourish in prosperous surroundings. Yet despite the relative degree of affluence, there seems to be certain common factors in the way suburbs sustain artistic life in their communities.

SURVEY OF FOUR SPECIFIC COMMUNITIES

Aside from general information about the arts in the suburbs, a special survey was made of four specific communities. Each of these communities maintains artistic identities of their own and furnishes financial support for their resident arts institutions. While sharing similar objectives, each of the four communities has evolved in a different way. Arlington, Virginia, is a suburban county just across the Potomac River from Washington, D.C. The county is the smallest political unit, with no further subdivisions. Palo Alto is located in Santa Clara, California, and is thirty-five miles from San Francisco. Technically it is a city. However, aside from the governmental context, it is a suburb of San Francisco in much the same manner that the "cities" of Long Island are suburbs of New York. Our third community is Huntington, New York. Forty miles from Manhattan, it is one of ten townships in Suffolk County and contains several incorporated villages. Bergen County, New Jersey, our fourth community, is just northwest of Manhattan and contains seventy towns or boroughs within its boundaries. The cities of Hackensack and Englewood are located in the county but they do not dominate it in any sense, for Bergen is overwhelmingly suburban in character. Situated in different parts of the country and having varied governmental structures, these suburban communities all have a commitment to the arts.

What Are the Arts?

The cultural life-style of the suburbs has a different emphasis from that of the city. While it remains true for both city and noncity dwellers that approximately 4 per cent of the total national population regularly attend museums, concerts, dance, and theater in the formal traditional sense, this percentage jumps to 48 per cent when audiences at rock and pop concerts and participants in crafts, visual arts, and amateur musical programs are included. The suburbs are particularly identified with these additional elements.

What constitutes the arts has always been open to passionate debate. We too long have accepted the notion of the arts as noble, revered, and housed in mighty surroundings. This canard has been reinforced with the construction of culture palaces for music, ballet, opera, theater, painting, and sculpture. However, the remarkable spread of rural crafts into the suburbs, the growth of art centers in suburban communities, and the proliferation of community orchestras, theaters, and rock ensembles have confounded the traditional interpretations of art. It would be foolhardy to draw lines; in the final analysis art is determined by whether it is good or bad, not by what form it takes or the location in which it is performed. As the report, "The Place of the Arts in New Towns," stated:

> The definition of the 'arts' is surely wider than a church door since it admits everything from preschool fingerpainting through school programs in esthetics or dance, through housewifely pot-throwing and one-man leather crafting to money-making rock concerts to the reaches of 'high' art in ballet and symphony.

In this essay the terms "professional" and "community" arts are frequently used. By "professional" the inference is that artists are financially compensated and the standard of their work is high. By "community" the implication is that the activity is conducted by amateurs and the standards are not equal to best professional levels. There are exceptions, of course; some community arts achieve very high standards and some professional arts, low standards. Artists associated with community groups referred to in this essay are invited to assume they are part of the worthy exception.

THE DECENTRALIZATION OF THE ARTS

Culture and especially the arts have usually been identified with large cities. However, mass media, mass higher education, and mass transportation have spread urban civilization throughout the nation. Isolated provincial life largely has been liquidated and there are no more "hicks" or "country bumpkins." With the spread of urban civilization, people outside of large cities desire cultural opportunities within their own communities. In part this cultural explosion is mere boosterism and civic pride—a way of getting the community on the map. But in a larger sense it is a genuine desire for a cultural alternative. The growth of the arts in suburbia is really part of a general decentralization of American society. People leave big cities because they prefer the kinds of lives they can live in smaller suburban communities or cities of modest size. However, they also desire the amenities of urban life in this setting.

Suburbia has been effected most by this desire and decentralization. Attuned by proximity to urban arts yet drawn emotionally to the land, the middle landscape becomes a rich blend of traditional urban arts such as symphonic music and rural crafts such as leather crafting. Since suburbia in this century has been identified with bourgeois tastes, one must add popular culture to the mixture. None of these elements dominate the arts in suburbia and all more or less coexist side by side.

INCOME LEVEL AND THE ARTS IN SUBURBIA

While rural crafts and imported rock concerts need little

encouragement in suburbia, the visual and performing arts traditionally associated with cities do. These are most highly regarded by middle- and upper-income suburban families. However, the arts do not command the same degree of attention for a majority of these suburban families as they do for their city counterparts. It is not that people in the suburbs have less interest in the arts, but rather that there is a shift of emphasis on what is important to them as they pass through the life cycle. The structure of city apartment life or suburban ranch-house life does not change, but the concerns of people within those structures do.

Middle- and upper-income families who live in city apartments do so for a variety of reasons, but principally to establish a commitment to their professional life, to be free of the responsibilities of home ownership and daily commuting, or to partake of the pleasures and cultural resources available in the city. The choice is often made with graceful acceptance of the hardships of urban life. Apartment living for the well-to-do suggests an adult-centered world.

When these same adults have lively children, the shift is from themselves to their family and here the suburbs offer distinct advantages over the city. Furthermore, ownership of property and the building of equity for future security become foremost in the thinking of many suburban parents. As Lee Howard, Director of the Huntington Arts Council stated, "People make a strong commitment to the maintenance of a home and land, and in being part of a community when they move to the suburbs. The self-gratifying pleasures of city arts experiences give way to undertaking community responsibilities, serving on PTAs, giving of one's time to church, school, and other community service."

To some degree the arts suffered in a traditional suburban environment because home ownership and child rearing prevented many individuals from devoting the time and energy required to foster them in their communities. However, the suburbs are changing. Garden apartments, condominiums, and apartment houses are becoming more popular in suburbia. This development and the recent infusion of diverse groups such as the elderly and single persons should help enrich the cultural life of the middle landscape. In addition, this distinction should not be overemphasized because there are homeowners in the city who share the sense of community and family that we equate with tract living in the suburbs, particularly in the blue-collar neighborhoods of the outer city. Both stress a life-style focused on home, church, and immediate neighorhood, which is often ethnic in character.

Such blue-collar neighborhoods, city or suburban, almost always are lacking in cultural opportunities and this is not the fault of the people who live there. The spontaneous leadership in the arts that occurs in higher-income communities is less likely to happen here. The existing neighborhood institutions—churches, lodges, and other organizations—have not been encouraged to develop cultural programs as part of their community service. In a Harris Poll conducted in 1973, one particular finding stressed that the single group most unhappy with the lack of nearby cultural opportunities were the blue-collar workers, that is, those individuals with high school educations and in the $5,000 to $15,000 income bracket. Their stratum of the population did not identify with the city core or the cultural center in the suburbs, but viewed their neighborhoods as the center of their life's activities. In this regard, the report stated:

> Many of the poor or poorly educated seem unaware of the facilities available to them, or perhaps worse, assume that the facilities are not for them. . . . The need for increased decentralization of the arts and culture seems to be borne out by the data.

ARTS VISIBILITY AND INDOCTRINATION

While there is cultural activity taking place in the suburbs, a casual traveler to these areas would be hard put to find clues that artists and orchestras are about. It is in the nature of the suburbs—spread out, geographically unfocused—that their arts activities are virtually hidden. The only human activity in evidence is what takes place on ball fields. The city cynic driving through the suburbs to his country retreat can easily dismiss a tract of split-level houses as further evidence of suburban wasteland. But little does he know of the art studios or potters' wheels that are tucked away in the basements of these houses, or of the chamber music workshop taking place in an unprepossessing school building.

A survey of eighty Arlington County artists revealed that thirty-eight had studios in their homes, another twenty-three had studios apart from their homes, and nineteen had no studios. When these artists leave their work area, they drive in automobiles to wherever they purchase supplies or attend to household needs. Few passers-by would notice them and fewer yet recognize them as artists. The low level of visibility of arts activity is perhaps one reason outsiders give a negative rating to the suburban cultural scene.

Compare this profile to that of the artist in a large city. He is visible. He might live in a distinctive neighborhood with other artists. There are areas in each major city where artists congregate. Moreover, there are centers where his work or that of his fellow artists are always on exhibition. The passing world sees him as an artist, and in many ways honors him as such.

Visibility also is a factor in the public buildings on the cityscape. From neoclassic nineteenth-century structures to the most avant-garde, they remain imbedded in the consciousness of the beholder. The Philadelphia Museum of Art, rising in Olympian fashion over the city, is one of the visual images that even the most underprivileged child from the north side retains of his city. Similarly impressive is the Palace of Legion of Honor in San Francisco. Examples from New York are almost too numerous to cite.

The fact that city children grow up with this presence might explain why vandalism and destruction, so often feared with art in open places, is minimal in cities but has occurred in one of New York's affluent suburbs. Except for instances of graffiti, most public art in New York City has escaped major damage. The only damage to the sculptures in Denver's

(Colorado) Burns Park is the deterioration from rain and sun. The park, once an abandoned field in a relatively depressed neighborhood, has become a haven for families, workers on lunch breaks, and young people. Compare this to Bergen County, New Jersey, where a Sculpture-in-the-Park exhibition in the principal county park had to be aborted in midsummer, 1974, because of wanton destruction and theft of art works.

The point here is that an art consciousness becomes part of the growth mechanism of a city child. He is exposed to a mixture of different people, variegated painted city walls, abstract public sculpture, and the classical architecture of old institutions. The suburban child must have these visual experiences imposed, through the schools, by field trips and, if he is lucky, by parents who provide the exposure. The liberalizing influences of the arts begin with years of quiet, constant exposure—through visibility, to participation, appreciation, and then understanding. The suburbs have to make up for what occurs naturally in the cities.

METHODS OF FOSTERING THE ARTS IN SUBURBIA

There are a number of ways in which suburbs compensate for the absence of spontaneous culturalization. The first is for a local college or university to assume an importance equal to that of the professional art centers in the city. In Palo Alto the Foothill and DeAnza Community colleges provide auditoriums which, in keeping with the Civic Center Act, are available to the community when not required by the colleges. Foothill College has an auditorium seating 970 people as well as galleries, a planetarium, and other facilities. DeAnza College includes the Flint Center for the Performing Arts, which serves both Palo Alto and San Jose with a 2,500-seat auditorium ideal for accommodating large group attractions. The San Francisco Symphony maintains a regular series there supported by residents of Palo Alto and San Jose.

The important university in the life of Palo Alto, however, is its own resident, Stanford University. For many years the events at Stanford were the only source of artistic life in Palo Alto until 1933 when the Palo Alto Community Theater was built. Even now, the University continues to be the provider of touring professional events and faculty programs. It cosponsors some activities with the Art Department of Palo Alto, including an arts and education program in a junior high school.

Another suburban college that has taken strong initiative in the development of arts and community services is Bergen Community College in Bergen County, New Jersey. The college serves as a residential base for seven local arts groups including the Bergen Philharmonic, the Bergen Youth Orchestra, and the Pro Arte Chorale, a nationally known choral group. The North Jersey Cultural Council also is housed on its campus. The college makes modest grants of $1,000 each to sustain the seven resident groups and office space is available rent free. There is yet no auditorium; however, future construction plans include a 2,500-seat facility comparable to that at the Flint Center to serve the needs of both the community and the college. Bergen Community College also provides facilitative services and cosponsors a festival costing $15,000 which includes dance and other group attractions. Another college in Bergen County, Fairleigh Dickinson University, sponsors a distinguished musical series presented in a 1,200-seat county high-school auditorium.

The State University of New York at Purchase in suburban Westchester County recently opened the Neuberger Museum on its campus. Henry Moore's large bronze sculpture is located outside the museum in seeming recognition of the lack of art in public places. This new museum, in an area of affluent suburban homes and cultural drought, has become the local focal point for important developments in the art world. Aside from providing centers for cultural activities, colleges and universities have helped disperse the arts throughout the nation by having resident writers, artists, sculptors, musicians, and dramatists who not only serve the students of these institutions but the community as well.

The recognition of the lack of spontaneous culturalization

among younger children has led to the development of school arts education programs. A number of school systems have adopted these programs which include performances, artists in residence, teacher workshops, and the like. It is increasingly recognized that programs which include limited experiences and a superficial introduction to the arts have little or no permanent effect on students. Specialists point out, too, that more damage than good may result when a performance of inferior quality is given before a horde of school children. By and large, though, frequent programs of artistic depth can provide the spoon-feeding needed for the student not reared in a cultural environment.

The suburbs have benefited from the federal government's active involvement in the arts. The National Endowment for the Arts (NEA) not only underwrites arts projects but also has been instrumental in dispersing cultural programs throughout the nation. NEA has funded such projects as Artrain which brings paintings to communities which have no museum of their own. The train also houses sculptors, silversmiths, and potters, who demonstrate their crafts.

In addition to federal funding, the state governments have begun to underwrite the arts. Many new arts facilities are still built in cities, but there is a trend to locate some of these facilities in suburban areas. This is especially true in the eastern half of the country, where urban arts institutions are well established and the need for facilities is greatest in suburban areas. For instance, the Garden State Arts Center in New Jersey, opened in 1973, is located on a major highway in a suburban area. Other centers recently opened are Art Park near Buffalo, Wolf Trap Farm Park near Washington, Blossom Music Center near Cleveland, and Meadowbrook near Detroit.

Every state now has an arts council which is designed to promote cultural activities. Many of these are new and have not made a great impact on the arts. Those that have still favor established urban institutions. Yet by their very nature, these state arts councils will cause a further decentralization of cultural pursuits.

The New York State Council on the Arts is the most advanced in the country. Its allocation of some $35.6 million in funds to state arts groups in 1974–75 is a record commitment. This is almost one half of the amount spent by the federal government for all the arts in the entire nation, and is seventeen times greater than the appropriation of the second highest state. Much of this money is funneled into established urban arts institutions but enough is dispersed through a per capita formula to other areas, including the suburbs, to foster cultural activities.

While school programs and government support are essential to the development of the arts in suburbia, ultimately it is the support individual communities give which will be of lasting effect. It is local groups who foster interest in the arts and develop programs for the community. The usual method is for a group of individuals to form a local arts council which acts as a liaison to federal and state agencies. Aside from seeking outside funding, the local arts council also develops community financing for their programs. Arlington County, Virginia; Huntington, New York; and Palo Alto, California are among the most advanced suburban communities in developing and financing local arts programs.

LOCAL FINANCIAL SUPPORT OF FOUR COMMUNITIES

Arlington County Performing Arts functions much as a private arts council—co-ordinating information, providing facilities, and the like—except for the fact that it is a governmental body. It is a section of the Recreation Division under the Department of Environmental Affairs and serves a population of 170,000. Presently, it addresses itself principally to the performing arts, but the needs of visual arts are under study. The performing arts section receives $200,000 of which $170,000 goes to nine arts groups in the form of program funds and to another four arts groups in the form of direct services, together with $30,000 to the administration of the section. The total figure represents a per capita expenditure of $1.18.

The four functions of the performing arts section are to initiate and develop programs in the performing arts; to act as a resource for the county in the performing arts; to act as a coordinating agency for performing arts groups in the county; and to represent the county in the use of public funds and facilities. The performing arts section also manages a county-owned theater in a junior high school and administers an arts and education program in the schools.

Unlike Arlington County, the Arts Department of Palo Alto is restricted in its function as a governmental agency and does not play the role of an arts council, nor is it part of another agency such as recreation and environmental affairs. The department, however, plays an important role through the management of several city-owned facilities for the arts and cosponsorship of programs with community arts groups.

Out of its budget of $325,000, $65,000 goes to a children's theater, $47,000 to a community theater, $25,000 to miscellaneous music and dance programs, and $73,000 for a cultural center and visual arts programs taking place in it. The balance of $115,000 goes to the administration of the department and cultural center, including the salaries of more than ten full-time employees. In terms of Palo Alto's population of 54,000, this represents a per capita allocation of slightly over $6.00 per person. In addition to this annual appropriation, Palo Alto has provided almost $500,000 during the past five years for capital projects. Other sums accrue to the arts directly or indirectly through other governmental departments. Local resources are extremely important here because the California State Commission of the Arts has not exhibited a proportional commitment to these cultural activities.

In New York, the Huntington Arts Council provides co-ordinating services characteristic of a community arts council for sixty-one member arts groups, serving a population of 200,000. The council exerts considerable influence on the town board in favor of budget allocations for local arts groups. In 1974–75 the town of Huntington approved $200,000 in support of these projects. This representing a $1.00 per capita allocation for the arts. Rather than allocating funds for buildings and maintenance, the town makes direct grants to arts organizations. In addition, the town recreation department provides funds for over eighty arts events in town parks during the summer. Huntington's arts groups are a model of governmental funding at all levels. In addition to the town's generous support, some groups receive funds from the New York State Council on the Arts for a total of $224,000, and in 1974 the County of Suffolk, of which Huntington is part, allocated for the first time $28,000 to the same Huntington groups.

With a population of one million, Bergen County, New Jersey, is the largest of these four communities but it provides the smallest direct support for the arts. Nevertheless, its $10,-000 grant to the North Jersey Cultural Council in 1974–75 represents the largest commitment of funds to the arts by any New Jersey county. In addition, the county provides indirect funds through the local community college. The arts in Bergen County therefore are heavily dependent on the college. This is in direct contrast to Huntington and Arlington which have no college or university to cling to. Palo Alto has a balanced program of college support and local funding.

ARTS PROGRAMS IN SUBURBIA

There is no consensus on what types of art programs should be encouraged in the suburbs. While the interests of the people in a particular community play some role in determining programs, it is usually the most influential personalities who tend to shape the character of the arts in a given community. This is as true in suburbia as in the city where arts institutions and artistic movements take on the hue of their most powerful exponents. Creative leadership—whether that of an artistic director or a president of the board—is the exponential factor in art. Art usually does not arise spontaneously from surging human need. It is presented by an individual and his followers to the people, for them to discover and to enjoy. In their creation, the arts are totally undemocratic and in their maintenance often autocratic.

A major emphasis in the suburbs is involvement, whether as performer, craftsman, student in workshops or adult education, manager of an arts group, or member of a board. This is not to say that such participation is not seen in cities. Rather it is to underscore that activities of this nature are secondary to attendance at professional performances or exhibitions in the urban life-style. In the city the box office is supreme, and success or failure of a city's artistic life is registered by box-office receipts or by head count at the museum gate. The suburbs, as Johnnies-come-lately to the arts scene, are not charged with the task of sustaining imposing and often costly institutions built by prior generations. Their programs will more than likely disregard head count for the measure of success some child, senior citizen, or adult might have with a piece of clay or sculpture wire. Building good audiences for professional arts can be done by building a knowledgeable audience through community participatory programs, and suburbanites seem well aware of this.

Arlington is eager to strengthen its community arts activities—its theater groups, chorus, orchestra—and to develop community-managed projects in other disciplines. Washington D.C.'s magnificent Kennedy Center and Arena Theatre provide the "local" professional activity which is complemented by Arlington's community resources. The participatory nature of the arts here is important, if not vital, for Arlington County is concerned principally with the personal fulfillment of its citizens. Almost urban in character, with two thirds of the population living in apartments and almost 11 per cent of its population senior citizens, Arlington is acknowledged to have the highest per capita income of any county in the United States. It is only twenty minutes from downtown Washington, and significantly its needs are not to import or create professional-level activities but to provide opportunities for its people to participate in a way they cannot in Washington. In Arlington, then, "art for art's sake," according to Norman Kaderlan, Director of Performing Arts, "is secondary to the individual's self-discovery through art."

Palo Alto's dedication to community arts is demonstrated

by its substantial allocations as mentioned earlier. Yet, Palo Alto is clearly aware of the need for professional standards in its community. First-rate performances are routinely available at Stanford University in Palo Alto proper. Still, the city senses a need to upgrade the level of presentations in its community. The needs of the nonparticipant must be weighed as carefully as those of the do-it-yourselfer. Allan Longacre, Director of Performing Arts in Palo Alto, believes that, "If a person's expectation is excellence and quality, he has a right to benefit from public funds by attending professional presentations just as the participant has the right to expect support for his community theater, art center, etc." Palo Alto tries not only to be responsive to both needs, but also to achieve the right balance. Through a unique method of contracting for service, the city is able to underwrite the use of facilities and equipment for amateur and professional activity alike.

Huntington, New York, prefers to create its own professional companies. The town fathers joined together to support the creation of full-time professional theater, a fully professional symphony, and a recently formed ballet company. The Heckscher Museum, housing several Dutch Masters as part of its excellent permanent collection, receives heavy municipal support and is, in fact, considering expansion. The development and sustenance of Huntington's arts resources more closely parallels those of a city than those of the other communities under discussion. However, the needs of the amateur are not overlooked. There is an active art league, a community orchestra, and many other do-it-yourself activity groups.

Aside from the desires of the community and the preferences of local leaders, suburban arts programs in part are determined by what the main city has to offer. As noted earlier, the availability of professional arts activity in Washington, D.C., encourages Arlington to emphasize community arts and de-emphasize professional activities. With Washington's National Symphony next door, Arlington's orchestra functions as a community orchestra and one of relatively high standards as community orchestras go. It has an extensive series of concerts and performs contemporary as well as traditional repertory. However, if there is a cultural void or limitation in the neighboring city, then the suburb usually will attempt to fill it. Arlington's only publicly performing professional organization is The Opera Theater of Northern Virginia which presents major performances of contemporary or unusual operas in the English language, executed in modest but tastefully designed productions. One of the major reasons it was formed is due to the fact that the resident opera company in Washington, D.C. performs a limited season and is often sold out.

In the visual arts, Arlington artists are pretty much on their own. The dominance of Washington's great art institutions and their immediate accessibility have more than fulfilled Arlington's thirst for the visual arts. This has left local artists high and dry, forcing them to put on their own shows and to seek space for exhibitions. Under the recreation division's organizational structure, the performing arts section does not serve a co-ordinating role in the visual arts, but it has hosted a study that recommends a stronger effort on behalf of Arlington's numerous gifted amateur and professional artists.

Huntington is not dissimilar to Arlington with regard to the visual arts. Dominated by the vast resources of New York City, the visual arts seem to play a secondary role to the performing arts despite the existence of the Heckscher Museum. This museum, given to the people of Huntington by the Heckscher family in 1935, displays the family's private collection in a handsome, classic marble structure. The Heckscher Museum does not have an active membership program comparable to that of city museums, nor does it sponsor arts activities or educational workshops in conjunction with its collection. It serves principally as an exhibition space for its own fine collection and for regular visiting shows. However, there are plans to develop services through a membership program.

In contrast, Palo Alto does emphasize the visual arts. In part, this is due to the fact that the visual arts are not an outstanding cultural attraction in San Francisco. Palo Alto created its first arts facility in 1933 and has continued to develop its plant resources. The principal facility here is a community theater, which has served as model for communities and universities around the country. The city also has constructed a children's theater, built in 1935, a stage-craft shop in 1973, and an art center or cultural center, as it is called. This was the old City Hall renovated in 1970 at a cost of $330,000 to house community and city-sponsored activities.

There are rotating exhibits in the four galleries, which cover the spectrum of visual arts experience. There also is a dance studio, rehearsal and meeting rooms, and arts and crafts workshop space. A small auditorium accommodates concerts, lectures, films, and supplemental programs related to the art exhibits. The auditorium also serves for meetings and rehearsals. Over one hundred volunteers serve as gallery guides, curatorial assistants, and in other capacities. The ferment of visual arts activity in Palo Alto is further increased by the Palo Alto Art Club, a nonprofit community organization with an annual membership of approximately 1,200. The Cultural Center Guild sponsors an annual arts festival in addition to the festivals presented by the arts department in the parks and occasional outdoor exhibits in downtown Palo Alto. The important art festivals attract as many as a hundred artists and estimates of the number of visitors on a typical Saturday afternoon vary from 500 to 2,500. The Palo Alto Art Department manages the Cultural Center space as an open resource to community artists, and brings in distinguished visual artists to conduct master classes for the community.

The dominant theater in Palo Alto, like Arlington, is community theater. It is housed in an excellent facility created for it in the community-center complex. Also a community opera group, the Westbay Opera, has been producing operas with Bay Area talent for nearly twenty years. However, Palo Altans must travel to San Francisco for professional theater and opera. Palo Alto's musical life is closely tied in with Stanford University and the community colleges. There are several excellent youth orchestras, but private financial support for the orchestras is embarrassingly low and most of the professional costs are borne through affiliations with the educational institutions.

While many suburban areas are concerned with participation and filling gaps in the cultural offerings of the neighboring cities, some have decided to compete with the cities in major arts activities. In 1949, despite New York's strong musical offerings, Huntington began to develop its own symphony orchestra. Following established musical tradition, they formed a town band and this sparked interest in the formation of a community orchestra. The orchestra developed at a steady rate until it became fully professional in 1974 with seventy musicians. Its growth was methodical, and deliberate, in order to reach a wider region of Long Island with as many as forty-six concerts. A grant of $100,000 from the New York State Council on the Arts together with $10,000 from the town of Huntington and $19,000 from Suffolk County toward a total budget of $300,450 aided in this transition. In the meantime many of the amateurs and part-time musicians who formerly played with the Huntington Symphony (now incorporated as the Island Orchestra Society) formed a fifty-piece community orchestra, the Huntington Philharmonia. The presence of a professional symphony and a community orchestra in one suburban area is notable.

In a similar spirit, professional theater was born in Huntington and now serves most of Long Island. The Performing Arts Foundation, which operates six nights a week from September to June, has become a recognized regional theater even though it is within commuting distance of Broadway. Grants of $30,000 from the State Council on the Arts, $10,000 from the town, and $17,000 from the county toward an overall budget of $463,555 have aided in abetting Long Islanders' taste for good theater.

VISITING ATTRACTIONS

The importation of professional artists and companies is an important feature of suburban cultural life. Federal and state agencies favor this approach. In 1973 the National Endowment for the Arts granted $900,000 to New York City dance companies, much of which was used to underwrite tours in other states. Visiting artists and companies allow suburban communities to provide professional attractions without having to maintain such costly projects on a continual basis. They also provide suburbanites an opportunity to see and hear quality presentations without having to travel to the city.

Some representatives of suburban arts groups tend to be suspicious of local organizations that import big name events because they feel that appearances of outside performers draws audiences away from local arts presentations. Moreover, audiences that only insist on "name" events are in effect seeking a guarantee of quality and professionalism. They tend not to support the home-grown product unless it can stand up in quality to the imported event. Arlington's opera and Huntington's symphony and theater may well meet that test. This attitude is characteristic of many suburban residents. They will neither risk an evening on a relatively unknown artist, no matter how promising, nor attend a play by an unknown playwright, nor come out to see the efforts of a new choreographer. There are, of course, exceptions and Palo Alto with its university influence seems to be one of them.

To date, this attitude has tended to discourage artistic experimentation or innovation in suburban areas. In this respect the suburbs have yet to provide the soil for creativity that the city does, except in certain cases where universities are involved. This point is forcefully illustrated by the popularity of dinner theaters in the suburbs. These depend heavily on Broadway or off-Broadway hits. By contrast, dinner or cabaret theater in New York, Chicago, San Francisco, and Los Angeles tends to go in the opposite direction, providing experimental and improvisational styles of theater. Yet as the arts mature in suburbia and the population becomes more diverse, one can expect a more creative environment to be developed.

CONCLUSION

The arts seem to be taking root in suburbia and will continue to grow as state and local arts councils become firmly established. It will be nurtured by state and federal aid in much the same way that FHA mortgage policy and the highway program helped to develop suburbia generally. The degree of commitment to the arts will depend on community leadership, local financing, and regional facilities. While suburbs will not challenge cities for cultural leadership, one can foresee a more creative role for suburbia. This is especially true in communities where a variety of housing types are available and the homogeneity of suburbia gives way to more diverse elements in the population.

Those who feel that the suburbs cannot nurture the arts should be reminded that the same was once said about major business concerns. Today suburban areas contain more people than cities or rural areas and almost have an equal number of jobs. The movement of people and businesses have created a need for culture in the middle landscape. Huntington, Arlington, and Palo Alto have proven that culture scaled down to the size of the community can work. In many respects they are the forerunners of what we can expect in other suburban areas.

However, unlike many other aspects of life, suburban and city cultural developments will never be totally separated. Suburban audiences will continue to support city cultural offerings and touring professionals will perform in suburban areas. By and large most suburban cultural activities will emphasize participation or activities lacking in nearby urban areas. One can only wish this movement well since it reunites city and suburb and will make the latter a more exciting place to live.

BIBLIOGRAPHY

THERE ARE NO published sources which deal specifically with the arts in suburbia. In part this is due to the fact that the study of suburbia in general is a comparatively new field of research. In addition, many individuals in the arts have tended to discount suburban cultural activities and instead continue to emphasize traditional city offerings. Therefore, much of the material for this essay was drawn from a special survey conducted by the author.

The reader who is interested in general material which relates to this topic should be prepared to peruse a wide variety of sources. The interrelationship of the arts and society are discussed in Gifford Phillips, *The Arts in a Democratic Society* (Santa Barbara, Calif., 1966); Raymond Williams, *Culture and Society* (Garden City, N.Y., 1960); and Robert N. Wilson, *The Arts in Society* (Englewood Cliffs, N.J., 1964). Alvin Toffler's *The Culture Consumers* (New York, 1964) deals with the "culture boom" of the 1960s and its implications, while Alan Levy, *The Culture Vultures* (New York, 1968), examines the mass merchandising of culture to a small but loyal public. Irving Kristol, "Urban Civilization and its Discontents," *Commentary*, 50 (July, 1970), 29–35, is an important article which in part deals with the general decentralization of American society.

There are a number of works which include material on the organization, finances, and facilities utilized by arts institutions. Ralph Burgard, "The Creative Community," a 1973 report issued by the Associated Councils on the Arts (ACA), provides guidelines for community arts and science programs in related facilities. Michael Straight, "Cultural Life in a Great Society," *New Republic*, 152 (March 13, 1965), 11–15, looks closely at the financial support necessary for arts organizations. Keith Martin, "Arts Councils and Cultural Growth," *Museum News* 39 (December, 1960), 28–31, also deals with local arts councils while David Dempsey

"Uncle Sam, the Angel," New York *Times Magazine* (March 24, 1974), surveys the work of the National Endowment for the Arts.

A number of works deals with the means individuals can utilize to make the arts more effective in community life. Bruce Cutler, *The Arts at the Grass Roots* (Lawrence, Kans., 1968) is a good starting point; also "The Place of the Arts in New Towns," a 1973 report issued by the Educational Facilities Laboratories, describes the aspirations of new towns in integrating the arts into the fabric of their community life. "The Arts and the Small Community" (University of Wisconsin, 1967) consists of a series of papers which deal with community arts concepts. Though much progress has been made since these papers were delivered, they nevertheless provide the fundamental thoughts and ideas which are part of any good local arts program today. These papers were printed in pamphlet form. Part I was edited by Michael Warlum, Ralph Kohlhoff, and Mary Jane Even. Part II was edited by George Bauer. Adolph S. Tomars, "The Citizen in the Role of Producer and Consumer of Art," *Arts in Society*, 1 (1966), 45–55, contrasts amateur artistic programs and professional activities from a sociological viewpoint.

William S. Moorhead reviews what various authors consider the national attitude toward the arts in "Citizen's Strategies for Strengthening the Role of the Arts in a Human Environment," *Arts in Society*, 6 (Summer–Fall, 1971) 576–79. Information on audiences and the arts is contained in a number of studies, "Americans and the Arts: A Survey of Public Opinion," a 1974 report commissioned by the ACA and conducted by the National Research Center of the Arts, Inc., a subsidiary of Louis Harris and Associates, is a detailed description of American attitudes which dispels many current notions. The full report contains voluminous statistical data. However, the reader can obtain an abridged version entitled "Americans and the Arts: Highlights from a Survey of Public Opinion," which is issued by the ACA and designed for quick reference and easy reading.

Another report, "Arts and the People" (1973) conducted

for the American Council for the Arts in Education, contains statistical data on the attitudes of New York State residents toward participation and attendance of arts events. Oliver Rea's article "Expanding Audiences for the Arts," contained in the 1965 ACA publication, *The Arts: A Central Element of a Good Society,* also is well worth reading. The role of the arts in leisure is covered in Sebastian De Grazia, *Of Time, Work and Leisure,* and August Heckscher, "Leisure and the Arts," *American Federationist,* 70 (June, 1963), 268.

An entire issue of *Trends* (August–September, 1973), a publication of the Park Practice Program, was devoted to the cultural uses of park space throughout the nation. "A Directory of Community Arts Agencies" (1974) issued by the ACA includes the names, addresses, and programming information on over 250 community arts agencies throughout the country. *Administration in the Arts* published by the Center for Arts Administration of the University of Wisconsin, 1973, is another handy reference source.

Unfortunately, there are few in-depth studies of local arts programs. "A Cultural Action Plan for Westchester County, New York," a report written in 1975 by Ralph Burgard for the ACA, summarizes a five-part program to strengthen existing cultural institutions in Westchester and explores new ways of bringing the arts and sciences to the people. Keith Martin's previously cited article, "Arts Councils and Cultural Growth," details some of the programs of Binghamton's Robeson Memorial Center. Alvin H. Reiss, "Neighborhoods and the Performing Arts," *City Almanac* 4 (December, 1969), describes activities in New York City which could well be applied to any small community. The best source of information on current activities at the community level is the *ACA Reports* which are published monthly.

ZONING OUT THE POOR
by Paul Davidoff and Mary E. Brooks

THE SUBURBANIZATION of America is an accomplished fact. The suburbs have become the new America. They are where more people now live, more than in cities and more than in the nonmetropolitan areas of the nation. It is quite likely that by the end of this decade more employed persons will find their work in the suburbs than in other areas. Because the story to be told in this essay is one of discrimination and hostility on the part of suburban communities, it is useful at the outset to observe that suburban growth in America has had many positive virtues. Suburban development has provided a preferred alternative life-style for millions of Americans; that is, for those free to make a choice. The suburbs have offered privacy, freedom from congestion, a relatively sound environment and, in many cases, advantages in terms of education, health, employment, and recreation. The suburbs also have offered a refuge for many—a place to run to in order to disassociate from classes and races in the population found undesirable. It is the separation between sectors of the population that has characterized suburban development that is the focus of this essay.

We live in a nation that appears deeply committed to maintaining wide-scale disparities in opportunities between economic classes and between racial groups. To an extent previously undreamed of in America, the wall which separates slum and suburb has become thick, high, and impenetrable. Legal institutions have been devised so that laws of

TABLE 1

POPULATION BY RACE IN CITIES AND SUBURBS OF
STANDARD METROPOLITAN STATISTICAL AREAS (SMSA)
IN 1960 AND 1970

	1960	1970	% of Change
Total U.S. Population	179,000,000	203,000,000	+ 13.3%
Total SMSA Population	120,000,000	139,000,000	+ 16.6%
Total Central City Population	60,000,000	64,000,000	+ 6.4%
Total Outside Central City			
(Suburbs)	60,000,000	76,000,000	+ 26.8%
WHITE			
SMSA	106,000,000	121,000,000	+ 13.9%
Central City	49,000,000	49,000,000	0.0%
Outside Central City	56,000,000	71,000,000	+ 26.1%
NEGRO			
SMSA	13,000,000	17,000,000	+ 31.6%
Central City	10,000,000	15,000,000	+ 33.1%
Outside Central City	3,000,000	4,000,000	+ 26.6%

TABLE 2

PER CENT DISTRIBUTION OF POPULATION BY
RACE AND INCOME IN CITIES AND SUBURBS OF
STANDARD METROPOLITAN STATISTICAL AREAS (SMSA)
IN 1960 AND 1970

	Metropolitan Total	Central Cities	Outside Central Cities
Population			
1960	100%	50%	50%
1969	100	45	55
Population by Race			
WHITES			
1960	100	47	53
1970	100	41	59
NON-WHITES			
1960	100	78	22
1970	100	77	23
Families Below			
Low Income Level			
1959	100	61	39
1970	100	60	40

SOURCES: U. S. Bureau of Census, *U. S. Census of Population 1960–1970,* Vol. I "Changes in Urban America," U. S. Department of Labor, Bureau of Labor Statistics, Tables, D-1 and D-3, 1969; "Income of Families and Persons in the United States," U. S. Bureau of the Census, *Current Population Reports,* Series P-60, No. 66, 1969; and Consumer Income, "Characteristics of the Low Income Population," 1970, *Current Population Reports.*

suburban communities which control the use of land and resources have become the servants of race and class separatism.

In the 1960s, the term "apartheid" began to be used to describe the *de jure,* as well as the *de facto,* methods employed to separate rich communities from poor, to protect rich Americans and their children from contact with poor and even middle-class Americans and their children, and to separate black Americans from white Americans. From an urban nation we have become predominantly a suburban one, and this shift of population and of life-style has helped to sharpen the race and class cleavages among us. Will the suburbs remain an exclusive preserve for white middle- and upper-middle-income families, or will they become open and available for citizens of all incomes and races? Inherent in this dilemma is whether minority citizens, as well as moderate- and low-income families, will be allowed to enjoy the attractive qualities which are characteristic of suburbia.

The answer to this question is of the greatest import to the future of urban America. Opening of opportunities to those who elect to choose them may give rise to a solution to the basic problems of urban poverty and discrimination. If opportunities for lower-income and nonwhite families to reside in the suburbs continue to be denied, then our society will confront to an even greater extent than it does today the development of the two-class society—one white and affluent, the other nonwhite and poor—that the Kerner Commission predicted back in the late 1960s. Tables 1 and 2 give some indication of the extent of this problem.

THE LOCATION OF LOW- AND MODERATE-INCOME HOUSING

The problem of low- and moderate-income housing has historically been viewed as a production problem. It generally was believed that as long as greater quantities of low- and moderate-income housing became available, the situation was improving. Even today we are forced to be concerned with

the production of housing since financing clearly has become
the single most burdensome obstacle to relieving housing
problems in metropolitan areas. However, there is a growing
realization that low- and moderate-income housing canno
merely be measured in terms of numbers but also must be
treated in terms of location. Providing a decent home in a
suitable environment for every American family is a goal tha
cannot disregard the location of that home. In 1969 the Presi
dent's Committee on Urban Housing (the Kaiser Commis
sion) concluded that:

> The location of one's place of residence determines the accessi
> bility and quality of many everyday advantages taken for granted
> by the mainstream of American society. Among these common
> place advantages are public educational facilities for a family's
> children, adequate police and fire protection, and a decent sur
> rounding environment. In any case, a family should have the
> choice of living as close as economically possible to the bread
> winner's place of employment.

Opening suburban areas to low- and moderate-income
housing is not the total solution to the housing crisis in the
United States. Massive effort, talent, and monies must con
tinue to be concentrated in the core areas of major metro
politan centers. Suburban areas cannot be the total solution,
but they are an important component of a metropolitan solu
tion. And heretofore, suburbs have been the part of that solu
tion least explored. The problem of low- and moderate-in
come housing is metropolitan in scope because the manner in
which metropolitan regions developed have, at least in part,
been responsible for the severity of this housing problem. The
unplanned, unchecked flight into the suburbs has concen
trated vast resources on increasing the prosperity of a selected
portion of the population. At the same time, an overwhelming
proportion of the population, less affluent, was increasingly
less able to pursue the same objectives and aspirations.

RESTRICTIONS ON LOW- AND MODERATE-INCOME HOUSING

There is considerable disagreement on the responsibility of suburban areas to respond to the problem of developing low- and moderate-income housing throughout metropolitan regions. The usual response of suburban communities to the possibility of future low- and moderate-income housing in their community falls into four general categories:

(1) a reaction to the families that are believed to be moving into those units;

(2) a reaction to the type of dwellings that is associated with low- and moderate-income housing;

(3) a fear of the fiscal impact on the community;

(4) the "why us?" syndrome.

Many suburban residents react to the kind of person they believe will inhabit low- and moderate-income housing. These reactions are the least openly discussed and are frequently tied closely with racial fears and prejudices. For most it is a transposition of an image of central-city ghettos and ghetto-dwellers to the suburban neighborhood. For many it is an image of the fatherless black family with too many children, probably living on welfare. There is a fear that such families will destroy the community and bring down property values of adjoining houses. This image is difficult to counter. Undoubtedly there are many families bearing some or all of those characteristics which are not only black, but white, Spanish-American, and others. Moreover, no one can guarantee what kind of family will move into a low- or moderate-income house just as no one can guarantee what kind of family will move into an upper-income house.

What is perhaps important to note is that there is a wide variety of persons in need of low- and moderate-income housing regardless of their race and that the traditional stereotype of the low-income resident no longer applies. The elderly are a prominent recipient of low- and moderate-income housing. Even if they already reside in a suburban community, many elderly people are frequently forced to leave because there is no housing available at prices which they can afford on a fixed income. Unless the elderly family or person is in a home which has been completely paid for and requires little upkeep, they may be forced to move to less expensive housing either in the city or a less affluent community. Students and young married couples, perhaps with young children, are other major groups presently excluded from communities that restrict low- and moderate-income housing units. Many suburban communities have noted a marked outmigration of young people into other areas. While there are undoubtedly many reasons encouraging this trend, the lack of housing at prices they can afford is one factor forcing them to move.

The lack of low- and moderate-income housing has also begun to affect other sectors of the population. The working class, for instance, is frequently restricted from moving into a community because of the lack of housing at prices they can afford. These families may be headed by a skilled worker or members of the local police force, teachers, and other municipal employees whose salaries do not permit them housing in many communities. The individuals or families living or needing a low- and moderate-income house include a high proportion of the population in the United States. Communities restricting the development of low- and moderate-income housing thus are excluding many kinds of people.

Reactions to the type of dwellings associated with low- and moderate-income housing center primarily around density and aesthetic questions. Most developers insist that if housing is to be constructed to reach the low- and moderate-income family it must be built in some form of attached units, either row houses, town houses, garden apartments, or multifamily housing as opposed to the single-family detached housing now predominant in most suburban communities. Attached housing, in fact, has increased in popularity for all income classes throughout metropolitan areas, primarily because of the rapid increases in land and construction costs. Yet the attached dwelling unit has other reasons for its popularity. For some, the increased density is attractive because it provides greater opportunity for community interaction and involvement. For others, the freedom from home and property maintenance is an attraction. For smaller families, the more effective and efficient use of space may be an attraction. Others, not ready to purchase a single-family home, may choose to rent or purchase a condominium.

Increased density is usually associated with the worse characteristics of central city neighborhoods: crime, filth, traffic, and pollution. Admittedly, there are instances where increased density is not advisable for very legitimate reasons: topographic restrictions such as soil or drainage problems or insufficient roads for increased traffic are two good examples. But these arguments, unfortunately, are used too frequently in situations where they are not applicable.

Construction techniques and options for developers are now advanced enough so that many of these fears are unfounded. The developer may choose to cluster housing in several areas and leave large spans of land open for recreation and open space. Communities such as Reston, Virginia, Columbia, Maryland, and Heritage Village, Connecticut, are frequently viewed as very well-designed, aesthetically pleasing developments, which used such techniques. Moreover, many of these techniques can be carried over to much smaller developments, so that the aesthetic response to such housing can be quite positive.

It will take some time to cleanse our memories of those high-rise jungles frequently associated with low- and moderate-income housing and to replace those images with the low-rise, well-designed residential developments increasing in number throughout the United States. High-rise developments, except where land prices prohibit any other type of development, are usually the exception today. In many areas of the county, high-rises are suggested only for the elderly or for families without children.

No argument against the development of low- and moderate-income housing receives greater attention than the fiscal impact it will have on the receiving community. Unfortunately, there is data to support either side of the argument and very little of this information can be characterized as un-biased objective research. However, techniques for measuring the cost-revenue or benefit of a development have improved considerably over the years. For most suburban communities, the tax system, primarily the real property tax, provides the rationale for exclusion of any land use or family that does not "pay their own way." The property tax supports the largest portion of municipal costs (primarily public education) and is regarded as a major factor in maintaining the status of the community. Aside from discriminatory features, such a fiscal policy is self-defeating. For instance, a 1968 League of Women Voters study in New Castle, Delaware, showed that local school costs were so high that a new house would have to cost $58,500 in order to yield enough taxes to educate the average number of children per household—$1,688 in taxes for 1.6 children. Clearly, such a policy (with educational expenses increasing every year) carried to its logical extreme will eventually exclude upper-middle-class families. Alternatives to the present tax system and its educational support must be seriously pursued.

Two recent studies have provided enormous clarity to the questions of multifamily housing and the fiscal burdens communities must bear as a result of permitting such development. The first study, "The Costs of Sprawl," estimates various costs for six different neighborhood types and six different community types. The results of the study show, with a remarkable degree of consistency, that: "'planning' to some extent [planning always refers in this study only to the compactness of a development or essentially to clustering], but higher densities to a much greater extent, result in lower economic costs, environmental costs, natural resource consumption, and some personal costs for a given number of dwelling units." The report specifies, among other factors, that the total capital costs per dwelling unit (including residential, open space recreation, schools, roads, utilities, and land) decrease with higher densities, that total capital costs likely to be borne by local governments are reduced as much as 62 per cent in denser developments and public operating costs may be reduced by 73 per cent, and that energy and water consumption may also be reduced by approximately 40 per cent in high-density developments.

The second study, prepared by the New Jersey County and Municipal Government Study Commission entitled "Housing and Suburbs," generally concluded that not only was the fiscal issue particularly likely to be misperceived in planning and development decisions but that these fiscal concerns also were not well served by such decisions. Of particular interest to us here is their conclusion that while there are fiscal constraints on certain types of development—such as a development with a disproportionate amount of three-bedroom units —most types of apartment development are "substantially more beneficial to the municipal fisc than are many of the generally more popular single-family developments." The Commission was unable to identify significant circumstances "under which multifamily development resulted in an incremental investment pattern any different from the development of single-family detached homes." These conclusions contradict the practice of communities to disallow multifamily developments because of its incremental impact on infrastructure especially in light of the fact that the aggregate single-family developments will in time "require precisely the same type and level of municipal investment."

Finally, there are a range of arguments that fall into a category we may call the "why us?" syndrome. These arguments are frequently voiced in one of three ways:

(1) central cities should handle their own problems;

(2) who says that low- and moderate-income families want to live in our community anyway?

(3) why don't you pick on some other community?

The problem of creating adequate housing for low- and moderate-income families cannot be solved solely by central cities since it has been reported that 99 per cent of the vacant land in the nation's twenty largest urban areas lies outside the core cities. Moreover, this problem in part was caused by the artificial division between central cities and surrounding suburbs. Cities thus had to bear the inordinate cost of housing and servicing groups forced to live there because other choices were denied them. With the location of low- and moderate-income housing playing an increasingly important role in the production of these facilities, suburban and outlying areas must respond as part of the metropolitan region. The vast resources in suburban land cannot be sheltered for the exclusive benefit of the rich and white nor can it be denied to persons of lower income or different races. Neither city nor suburb is solely responsible for the problem and, therefore, neither should be solely responsible for the solution.

A number of studies have attempted to document the desire of central city residents to live in suburban communities or outlying areas. Preference and attitudinal studies are extremely difficult to conduct; however, most of these studies indicate a sizable portion of their respondents would choose an alternative location outside the central city. A study conducted in Dayton, Ohio, showed that "of the total sample, 51 per cent preferred a new home in their own neighborhood —and 44 per cent preferred a new home in the suburbs; 5 per cent were indifferent as to location. . . ." A study conducted for St. Paul, Minnesota, shows that 36 per cent of the black families in the area would prefer to live in a suburban location, whereas only 7 per cent do. A study completed for Cleveland, Ohio, showed that 20 per cent of the central-city residents would prefer suburban locations. Those persons interested in opening opportunities for low- and moderate-income families want to increase housing options for these groups so that they are no longer restricted to environments they find unsatisfactory. Families will not be forced from the central city to suburban locations; but, if they desire, they should have the option to move.

Because so much of the suburban exclusionary zoning issue has been focused on the legal battles in the courts, many communities feel discriminated against, as if they have been chosen, without justification, to assume a burden of the low- and moderate-income housing supply, while others remain free of such responsibility. The fact is that due to legal arguments involved, the battle against exclusionary zoning has been forced to proceed community by community.

How Communities Restrict Low- and Moderate-Income Housing

While there are many techniques communities can employ to restrict the development and construction of low- and moderate-income housing, the most important methods relate to zoning. Probably the earliest discussions about exclusionary zoning focused on large-lot zoning. Since that time the techniques employed by municipalities to exclude low- and moderate-income housing have gained in sophistication and complexity. The problem is compounded because many of these devices may be used quite legitimately for purposes other than the restriction of low- and moderate-income housing. Consequently the definition of exclusion has advanced to include the use of those techniques which have the effect of excluding low- and moderate-income housing whether or not the intent to do so is present. Zoning restrictions affect the ability of low- and moderate-income persons to move into a community primarily in three ways:

(1) *Restrictions as to the type of dwelling units permitted.* Residential development in the community may be limited to single-family units which are generally considered more expensive to construct than multifamily units.

(2) *Provisions which add to the cost of the dwelling unit.* Primary and secondary requirements which add to the cost of constructing the unit are those provisions which are in excess of what is considered necessary to protect the health, safety, morals, and general welfare of the public.

(3) *Administrative or procedural decisions which affect residential development.* There are a variety of decisions, controls, and delays which a community may exercise that work to lessen the desirability and/or feasibility of developing multifamily dwelling units.

Many zoning ordinances restrict the type of residential dwelling permitted to single-family detached houses. This effectively excludes any type of multifamily unit, such as town houses, row houses, garden apartments, duplexes, or multifamily units. Prohibition of these types of dwelling units will generally exclude low- and moderate-income families and minorities from the community because they cannot afford the more expensive types of housing. In addition, many zoning ordinances do not permit mobile homes or permit them only in undesirable rural or industrial areas. Mobile homes also can be excluded in indirect ways, for example, by imposing minimums relating to floor area, height, or other factors which this type of housing cannot meet. Because mobile homes tend to be less expensive units, their exclusion is another way of restricting the housing possibilities for low- and moderate-income families. Many requirements have the effect of controlling density, that is, the number of dwelling units permitted on a given unit of land. Lot sizes and yard requirements also are generally used to control density. These requirements, moreover, have the effect of restricting the development of the land because multifamily dwellings usually cannot be constructed with very low densities.

Large-lot zoning (frequently considered to be any minimum lot size over one-half acre per unit) is one of the principal provisions which adds to the cost of the dwelling unit and therefore is one of the most common types of exclusionary requirements. The 1962 "Spread City" report of the Regional Plan Association pointed out that in 1960 two thirds of the vacant land in the New York region (New York City plus four suburban counties) was zoned for lot sizes of more than one-half an acre, while less than one per cent was zoned for multifamily housing.

Large-lot zoning affects the cost of housing in a variety of ways. In 1968, the National Commission on Urban Problems (the Douglas Commission) stated that extensive large-lot zoning in a given area has the effect of substantially reducing the total amount of housing that can be accommodated, which will increase the costs of land generally. The Commission believed that the increase in the total house-and-lot price may be greater than the increase in land price because most

builders simply will not build a small house on a large lot believing that it is necessary to obtain a proper return on their
investment. Moreover, large-lot zoning generally results in
added costs for land improvements, such as linear feet of
streets, sidewalks, gutters, sewer and water lines. It also
should be noted that other restrictions such as excessive yard
requirements have the same effect as large-lot requirements;
front yard, side and rear yards, setbacks, frontage requirements are the most common ones. Less frequently seen are
those which require that the size of the house can occupy no
more than a certain proportion, such as 40 per cent, of the
total lot.

Other ordinances such as minimum floor-size restrictions
are claimed to be for the protection of the safety and health
of the residents. However, these devices have been carried to
extremes such as the one the Douglas Commission found in
Bloomington, Minnesota, a suburb of the Twin Cities area
where 1,700 square feet minimums were required, and, at a
square-foot construction cost of $15.82 (the average for
FHA Section 203 housing in the area), the smallest house
permitted would cost $26,894 in construction costs alone. If
such ordinances are required, they should not exceed the minimum established for health and safety. The most recent ap-
praisal of this minimum established to date is contained in a
proposed Model Housing Maintenance and Occupancy Ordinance prepared by the American Public Health Association.
This report stated that one hundred fifty square feet of floor
space are necessary for first occupancy and at least one hundred square feet of floor space for every additional occupancy
with the total number of persons equal to no more than two
times the number of its habitable rooms. If a minimum requirement of any sort is established, then there is virtually no
justification for that requirement to vary for different districts
within the ordinance or to vary for different types of dwelling
units. A minimum established for the health and safety of the
residents should be the same for all residents.

Many communities have excessive secondary restrictions
within their building codes. With increasing frequency

developers are being required to install or provide certain improvements long ago provided by municipal governments such as streets, schools, and parks, garages, off-street parking, accessory buildings, and landscaping. Some communities have "look-alike" or "nonlook-alike" ordinances which will either limit certain designs in that community or will not permit certain common features to appear too frequently. These restrictions also have the effect of increasing the final cost of constructing the dwelling unit.

The most sophisticated devices conceived to restrict low- and moderate-income housing and the most difficult to detect probably fall into the category of administrative or procedural delays. Richard Babcock and Fred Bosselman in their book, *Exclusionary Zoning: Land Use Regulation and Housing in the 1970s,* stated:

> The structure of land-use regulation is so confused with a labyrinth of semi-independent reviewing agencies that delay is inherent. Development in a typical community may involve the planning board, the zoning commission, the board of adjustment or zoning appeals, the building inspector, the zoning enforcement officer, the health department, the fire department, the water and sewer authorities, and the engineering department, not to mention other local boards which are indirectly affected such as the school board, the traffic department, the park and recreation department and so on.

OTHER EXCLUSIONARY TECHNIQUES

Aside from zoning, there are other techniques used for exclusion. Caution again must be exercised in understanding that many of these devices are not *always* employed as an exclusionary measure yet may be identified here as having an exclusionary effect on the construction of low- and moderate-income housing within a suburban community. Most of these land-use controls are similarly granted through the police power to the municipality to protect the health, safety, morals, and welfare of residents. We are concerned with those provisions which exceed requirements necessary for that protection. Such provisions unnecessarily add to the cost of the dwelling unit, add to the cost of improving the land upon which the unit is placed, or add to the final cost of the unit through procedural or administrative requirements. These provisions are generally found in subdivision ordinances, building codes, housing codes, and other codes and ordinances which may govern the construction of streets, sanitary and storm sewers, water and electric power, or facilities reserved for public use. A 1971 report of the Joint Task Force on Housing in Fairfax County, Virginia, stated that over $5,000 could be saved on a single-family residence designed to sell for $28,000 if unnecessary expenditures were eliminated in the cost of the unit and the cost of improving the land for that unit. The National Commission on Urban Problems report, "Building the American City," identified nearly $2,500 of code item costs beyond necessary minimums.

Major cost-inducing factors in the improvement of land are often found in the subdivision ordinance. The requirements of subdividing into individual lots for individual housing unit construction adds to the cost of development through the need for excessive grading, extensive utility lines, increased pavement of streets and sidewalks. Many subdivision codes do not permit the construction of any type of dwelling unit but the single-family detached house. Moreover, many subdivision ordinances are vague and such wording often permits municipalities to extract major commitments from the developer in exchange for approval of the proposed development.

Administrative fee requirements also add to the cost of housing units. Fees are usually required for building permits, certificates of occupancy, filing of variances, special permits, or planned-unit-development (PUD) applications. Moreover, a municipality may limit the number of building permits which can be obtained at any one time, requiring the developer to apply for additional permits each time the limit is reached in construction. Requirements for on-site inspections may prevent less expensive assembly of units elsewhere. Frequently a bond or cash deposit is required of the developer, necessitating larger loans and greater interest payments.

We have listed some of the regulations which *can* be exclusionary because they exceed minimum standards required for protecting the health, safety, morals, and welfare of residents. Admittedly, it is difficult both to isolate the regulations which can be restrictive and to identify at what point a regulation is excessive. For instance, architectural controls are frequently alleged to have a restrictive influence on housing construction adding to the cost of building the unit. Yet many suburban communities are not willing to permit proposed developments which have no amenities beyond minimum standards necessary to protect the health and safety of residents desiring more attractive neighborhoods. Are these regulations restrictive and at what point? The requirement of fees is often cited as a restrictive requirement, yet such fees are necessary to handle the administrative mechanism to approve development and construction. Many similar examples exist illustrating the difficulties in identifying the restrictiveness of provisions.

Most requirements, even those necessary to protect the health and safety of residents, add to the cost of constructing the dwelling unit. Much additional research is necessary to identify the degree of restrictiveness induced by such provisions. To date, we can merely increase the awareness of officials that such provisions should be reviewed to ascertain their restrictiveness on housing construction. However, a strong argument has been made for municipalities to adopt development ordinances combining all construction and development codes and ordinances into one document. As the report "Building the American City" points out, the multiplicity of controls over development dissects the construction and development process so that no comprehensive treatment is made of the environment and the dwelling. As a result technical and policy conflicts occur among the various codes and ordinances.

MEASURING EXCLUSIONARY ZONING

When a suburban municipality is accused of practicing exclusion against low-income, moderate-income, and minority groups, the reaction of its residents is often one of bewilderment. Such a community has often been guiding its development in a manner that seemed not only desirable, but "natural." It is sometimes a shock to discover that such aesthetically pleasant practices as large-lot zoning have the incidental effect of excluding from residence the bulk of the American population. For many suburban municipalities, the "natural" patterns of zoning and planning have prevailed, even when they have been socially destructive, because they have gone virtually unchallenged. One of the reasons for identifying exclusionary patterns is to move communities toward a better understanding of "inclusionary" zoning. This would show a municipality what actions it could voluntarily take within its zoning powers to remove restrictions and to develop into a more balanced and integrated community. Further, the objective of revising land-use regulations is to assure that community health, safety, and amenity requirements can be achieved without the racial and social-class discrimination that has resulted from the present practices.

Frequently, on the basis of the zoning text alone, local ordinances do not appear to be exclusionary. The planning division for Plainfield, New Jersey, prepared a report in 1971 entitled "Suburban Zoning Practices Surrounding Plainfield" which outlined suburban zoning practices in the hope of effecting a change in exclusionary practices. After documenting the population, industrial growth, income, and residential land uses in the suburban areas which surround Plainfield, they concluded that restrictive zoning practices usually occur in many suburban communities when the following conditions exist:

(1) If the community is in close proximity to a central city containing unemployed or underemployed workers.

(2) If the community has an employment base which is

growing and contains a number of unfilled jobs requiring unskilled and semiskilled workers.

(3) If the community has an already existing supply of moderate-income single-family homes, and requires new single-family homes to be constructed on large lots of one-half acre or more.

(4) If there is a limited amount of land, or no land, zoned for multifamily development.

(5) If there are financial resources which could be raised and made available for administrative costs and land purchase.

There have been attempts to correlate employment opportunities and housing opportunities as a measure of exclusion. The most detailed of these thus far has been the Fels Center Study, "Standards for Housing in Suburban Communities Based Upon Zoning for Work." The amount of land zoned for manufacturing, commercial, or other places of work were used to define standards for housing types to be included in a community. However, we believe that the amount of various types of residential districts cannot be determined from the amount of land zoned for various employment opportunities. If this were true, those suburban communities with little or no industrial or commercial space would have no obligation to build certain housing types. Yet such bedroom communities may offer better locations for workers in nearby communities and should respond to such locational advantages. Moreover, the more precise question is whether or not a family employed by a community or within that community can afford to live there based on incomes and the cost of housing within the community. Finally, the true intent of removing exclusionary practices is to provide an opportunity for *all* persons, regardless of their class or race, to live within a community. While access to employment opportunities is important as well as the opportunity to live and work in the same community, the right to live within a community cannot be dependent upon one's working within that community.

Quotas to End Exclusion

Some attempts have been made to establish quotas for low- and moderate-income housing to assist in determining at what point communities should no longer be obligated to provide a fair share of adequate housing. These programs are primarily aimed at encouraging a certain amount of low- and moderate-income housing within each community. The efforts make no attempt at determining exclusion, per se; they merely state that if low- and moderate-income housing does not exist to an established degree, the community is in effect exclusionary. A simple standard or quota for "integration" was established in 1969 in the case of *Gautreaux* v. *Chicago Housing Authority*. The Federal District Court for the Northern District of Illinois ordered the Chicago Housing Authority to build public housing in a ratio of three units in white neighborhoods for each unit in a nonwhite neighborhood.

The planning department for the city of San Francisco applied a different criterion for public housing within the city. Each planning district's ratio of public housing to total housing units must match the ratio for the city as a whole. In 1969, the Massachusetts State Legislature passed the Massachusetts Law for Low and Moderate Income Housing, frequently called the "Anti-Snob Zoning Law." This law was intended to stimulate the construction of low- and moderate-income housing throughout the cities and towns of Massachusetts. It provided relief from local zoning, building, and other codes for a public housing authority, nonprofit corporation, or a limited-dividend corporation by permitting the submission of a single application for the construction of subsidized housing. While the details of the law are not important here, a community may deny subsidized housing if to do so is "consistent with local needs." This is generally considered to be the case if more than 10 per cent of the community's existing housing stock are subsidized units, or when more than 1.5 per cent of the total land in the community, excluding publicly owned land, is devoted to subsidized housing. Proposed subsidized housing also may be denied if it will compromise more than 0.3 per cent of the land area in a community zoned for residential, commercial, and industrial use, excluding publically owned land, or ten acres, whichever is larger, during any one calendar year.

Other quotas have been established through the many "fair share" or allocation plans developed throughout the United States by planning agencies, councils of government (COG), and regional commissions. Such plans have been developed for the Dayton region in Ohio; Metropolitan Washington, D.C., COG; San Bernardino County, California; Denver Regional COG, Colorado; and St. Paul–Minneapolis, Minnesota. Many other areas are in various stages of developing such plans. Many of these housing plans allocate to planning areas throughout the region a certain number of low- and moderate-income or public and subsidized housing units as that area's "obligation" of the total regional housing need. While communities may not be labeled as exclusionary if this need is not met, meeting this "obligation" relieves them of further responsibility for low- and moderate-income housing until such time that the plan should reallocate a greater need.

The objection to establishing quotas is that once the quota has been reached the community essentially is relieved from any further obligation to house low- and moderate-income persons. They may then employ any exclusionary tactics they desire, because their quota has been met. They have no further responsibility to the low- and moderate-income families within the region or those who work within their own municipal borders. While the quota plans have achieved some very laudable objectives, particularly in reducing community opposition and in co-ordinating and implementing the construction of low- and moderate-income housing, we do not believe that any community should have an "out" which is reached when a certain number of units have been "put up with." The obligation of a community to be open and accessible to all persons, regardless of race or income, does not end at some arbitrary point. Certainly the enactment of public plans, policies, and laws cannot result in restricting housing opportunities for any person. The basic right of low- and moderate-income and minority persons to have free and equal housing locational choices should bear no limits.

THE MOVEMENT FOR OPEN SUBURBS

Over the past decade a growing, but still small, movement has been mounted by individuals and groups dedicated to opening up the suburbs. The reasons propelling their action may be as diverse as those who have imposed extreme restrictions on suburban development. The movement had its genesis in a host of housing and zoning cases involving the most blatant forms of racial restrictions. Examples of these include the zoning of blocks or districts by race (a practice declared unconstitutional in 1917 by the U. S. Supreme Court in the case of *Buchanan* v. *Warley*), and the use of private restrictive covenants to bar racial minorities from neighborhoods (a practice declared to be unenforceable under the Constitution by the U. S. Supreme Court in 1948 in the case of *Shelly* v. *Kramer*). In the last years of the 1960s a number of organizations turned their attention to the problems of suburban exclusion including the National Committee Against Discrimination in Housing which had been a leader in the fight for fair-housing legislation. The National Association for the Advancement of Colored People's director, Roy Wilkins, announced at a conference in December, 1969, that suburban discrimination would be the next battleground of the civil rights movement. His comments were made at a meeting jointly sponsored by the NAACP and the then recently created Suburban Action Institute (SAI). Suburban Action was organized for the specific purpose of expanding the rights of racial and economic minorities to reside in locations of their choice, including the suburbs.

The focus on suburban opportunities for minorities grew in significant measure as a response to federal programs aimed at rebuilding ghettos. Civil rightists and civil libertarians while supporting federal assistance to minority families were opposed to requirements that assistance be largely limited to ghetto areas. Ghettos were seen as conditions of constraint. Removing the constraint on locational opportunity by affording minorities choice of location throughout a metropolitan region including the suburbs would terminate the ghetto condition of an area.

The agencies organized to open the suburbs to minorities have pursued activities that have included research, organization, and administrative and legal action. The research has focused on demonstrating the existence of suburban exclusion and on describing new patterns of "inclusionary" development. Organizational work has aimed to create an enlarged group of advocates of open suburbs. The New Jersey Housing and Land Use Coalition and the Connecticut Coalition for Open Suburbs represent the product of organizing efforts. Important as educational and organizational activities are, by far the most decisive component of the open-suburbs movement has been that work which tested discriminatory suburban zoning in the courts. It has been the feeling of those who have been in the movement to open the suburbs that litigation was the only means that could successfully bring about a change in suburban zoning practices. It is still generally believed that remedial local or state legislation will not be forthcoming in any meaningful sense without the pressure of a judicial mandate for elimination of discriminatory zoning.

THE MOUNT LAUREL DECISION

We conclude that every such municipality must, by its land use regulations, presumptively make realistically possible an appropriate variety and choice of housing. More specifically, presumptively it cannot foreclose the opportunity of the classes of people mentioned for low- and moderate-income housing and in its regulations must affirmatively afford that opportunity, at least to the extent of the municipality's fair share of the present and prospective regional need therefor. These obligations must be met unless the particular municipality can sustain the heavy burden of demonstrating peculiar circumstances which dictate that it should not be required so to do.

With this powerful statement of the obligation of munici-palities to meet the housing needs of low- and moderate-in-come persons, the New Jersey Supreme Court (the highest court in that state) in its decision in the case of *Southern Burlington County NAACP et al.* v. *Township of Mount Laurel* (hereinafter referred to as the Mount Laurel case) has handed down the most far-reaching opinion on exclusionary zoning yet evidenced in years of litigation on this issue.

Mount Laurel is a developing community characterized by open farmland. However, it is crisscrossed by major highways and has become the home of a number of large industrial plants. Nearly 30 per cent of the Township's land is zoned for industry. The residential land area has been zoned to permit only single-family detached dwellings. Mount Laurel's resi-dential areas, therefore, have an almost all-white complexion even though its population grew from 2,817 in 1950 to 11,221 in 1970 and the Township lies adjacent to the city of Camden which has a primarily black and Puerto Rican popu-lation. In general, Mount Laurel's ordinance requirements are characteristic of many suburban communities surrounding major metropolitan centers which, as the Court stated, "real-istically allow only homes within the financial reach of per-sons of at least middle income."

The court recognized many of the problems inherent in exclusionary practices which prevail in suburban America. It found that specific regulations in Mount Laurel's zoning ordi-nance were "presumptively contrary to the general welfare and outside the intended scope of the zoning power." Those zoning measures discussed were Mount Laurel's exclusion of all types of dwelling units except single-family detached houses, bedroom restrictions, minimum-lot area, lot frontage, building size, and large amounts of land zoned for industrial and related uses. Each of these was discussed by the Court in terms of its restrictive effect on low- and moderate-income households.

The Court reached its decision under the state constitution and did not consider federal constitutional questions. Nonetheless, the Court stated that all enactments of the state's police power, which provides for land-use regulation, "must conform to the basic state constitutional requirements of substantive due process and equal protection of the laws . . . the requirements of which may be more demanding than those of the federal Constitution." The Court also stated "it is required that, affirmatively, a zoning regulation, like any police power enactment, must promote public health, safety, morals or the general welfare." The basic importance of housing and local regulations restricting its availability to substantial segments of the population falls within matters of constitutional dimension. The Court noted that "if a zoning regulation violates the enabling act with respect to the general welfare, it is also theoretically invalid under the state constitution."

In discussing the general welfare, the Court recognized that it is the municipality's responsibility to make provision for low- and moderate-income housing. The decision stressed a "nonlocal approach" in cases of zoning where there is broad public benefit as distinct from purely parochial interest. The Court stated that:

> It is plain beyond dispute that proper provision for adequate housing of all categories of people is certainly an absolute essential in promotion of the general welfare required in all local land use regulation. Further the universal and constant need for such housing is so important and of such broad public interest that the general welfare which developing municipalities like Mount Laurel must consider extends beyond their boundaries and cannot be parochially confined to the claimed good of the particular municipality. It has to follow that, broadly speaking, the presumptive obligation arises for each such municipality affirmatively to plan and provide for an appropriate variety and choice of housing, including, of course, low- and moderate-cost housing, to meet the needs, desires, and resources of all categories of people who may desire to live within its boundaries. Negatively, it may not adopt regulations or policies which thwart or preclude that opportunity.

The Court clearly recognized the importance of a well-defined regional plan to guide the development and the provision of housing opportunities for citizens throughout the region. The Court discussed the definition of a region, stating that the composition will vary from situation to situation but that confinement to a county appears unrealistic. Restriction to the boundaries of the state might be practical, the court stated, but a municipality may not disregard housing needs of persons who commute to another state. Nonetheless for Mount Laurel, the Court defined the region as those areas "within a semicircle having a radius of 20 miles or so from the heart of Camden City." The Court recommended specific zoning changes in the Mount Laurel decision. These included:

permitting multifamily housing, without bedroom or similar restrictions,

permitting small dwellings on very small lots,

permitting low-cost housing of other types,

permitting high-density zoning without artificial and unjustifiable minimum requirements as to lot size, building size, and the like,

permitting adequate housing within the means of employees of industry and commerce for which the municipality has zoned,

permitting within allowed planned-unit developments a reasonable amount of low- and moderate-income housing in its residential mix, and,

permitting an amount of land for industrial and commercial purposes reasonably related to the present and future potential for such purposes.

The Court proceeded to discuss the reasons put forth by Mount Laurel to justify its zoning provisions and in doing so made a strong statement against fiscal zoning. A developing municipality may properly zone for ratables to create a better economic balance for itself, according to the Court, provided that it is "done reasonably as part of and in furtherance of a legitimate comprehensive plan for the zoning of the entire municipality." But the Court invalidated municipal exclusion by zoning out types of housing and kinds of people for that same local financial end. The Court stated: "We have no hesitancy in now saying, and do so emphatically, that, considering the basic importance of the opportunity for appropriate housing for all classes of our citizenry, no municipality may exclude or limit classes of our citizenry, no municipality may exclude or limit classes of housing for that reason or purpose." The Court fully recognized the burden on municipalities to meet municipal costs but stated that relief from the consequences of our tax system will have to be furnished by other branches of government. "It cannot legitimately be accomplished by restricting types of housing through the zoning process in developing municipalities." In other words, communities such as Mount Laurel must zone primarily for the living welfare of people and not for the benefit of the local tax rate.

Conceding that environmental factors were important, the Court stated that "only a relatively small portion of a developing municipality will be involved, for, to have a valid effect, the danger and impact must be substantial and very real . . . not simply a makeweight to support exclusionary housing measures or preclude growth—and the regulation adopted must be only that reasonably necessary for public protection of a vital interest." The lack of water and sewer facilities in Mount Laurel, where land is amenable to utility installations, was not sufficient excuse for limiting housing to single-family dwellings on large lots, according to the Court. The Mount Laurel case will affect other developing communities in New Jersey. The Court deliberately stated that this decision is applicable to other municipalities which are:

. . . of sizable land area outside the central cities and older built-up suburbs of our North and South metropolitan areas (and surrounding some of the smaller cities outside those areas as well) which, like Mount Laurel, have substantially shed rural characteristics and have undergone great population increase . . . but still are not completely developed and remain in the path of inevitable future residential, commercial, and industrial demand and growth.

The Mount Laurel decision is the most encouraging sign to date that exclusionary suburban zoning practices are being recognized as discriminatory. It has given full support to those who have claimed that suburban growth policies have been misapplied to benefit the fiscal base of the community and the families privileged to live within its borders. Soon after the Mount Laurel decision was delivered, groups in New York and Connecticut announced plans to challenge exclusionary suburban practices in their state court systems. No doubt, similar court action will commence in other states as well. The Mount Laurel decision exemplifies the fact that the judiciary is still far more willing than state and local governments to solve this and other civil rights issues.

THE BALANCED COMMUNITY: AN IMPROVED LIFESTYLE

Land becomes an even more critical resource as metropolitan regions become more involved with concepts of large-scale developments and residential communities with a mixture of housing types and varied residents. As land-use controls begin to reflect concern for low- and moderate-income housing development, such housing begins to play a more integral part in the future development of metropolitan areas. A balanced community occurs when in the residential portion of a community or development, a variety of housing types and prices permit a socioeconomic and racial mix of residents to live there. The degree to which the balanced community should be the subject of public regulations has received considerable debate. Experts have concluded that in no case should the unresolved legal questions focusing on the balanced community justify denying access to housing. Nonetheless, the degree to which regulations should induce the balanced communities is unclear. At any rate, a variety of zoning provisions are appearing which encourage, if not require, the development of mixed residential communities. Such regulations place an even greater premium on the locations available for such development.

Several communities throughout the United States already have adopted or have given consideration to the adoption of provisions which give developers some incentive for including low- and moderate-income housing within the development proposed. Fremont, California; New Castle, Delaware; Arlington County, Virginia; Lakewood, Colorado; and Montgomery County, Maryland, are a few areas which have given attention to such provisions. More importantly, an increasing number of communities has also begun to consider requiring the developer to include a certain amount of low- and moderate-income housing in the total development. Fairfax County, Virginia, has received the most attention for its provisions in this area. Montgomery County, Maryland; Los Angeles, California; Denver, Colorado; St. Paul, Minnesota; DuPage County, Illinois; Cherry Hill, New Jersey; Lewisboro, New York, and several other areas also have given consideration to such provisions.

Existing suburban communities have not provided a completely satisfactory way of life. As Richard Babcock and Fred Bosselman pointed out, "It is the children of the McLeans and the Grosse Pointes and the San Leandros of this nation who are rebelling most destructively against the environment in which they were 'privileged' to grow up." Irving Kristol has summed it up perfectly in the title of his essay "The Young are Trying to Tell Us Something About Scarsdale." Therefore, the inclusion of various income and racial groups into suburban communities should not be viewed solely as a burden to be borne by their present residents. This trend will not only benefit minority groups but also the present residents and the community as a whole. Population heterogeneity will provide cultural diversity which in turn will enrich everyone's life. This will promote tolerance of social and cultural differences, thus reducing conflict among various groups in American society.

Higher density in well-planned multiple-family developments also will add economic advantages to suburban communities by the addition of more consumers in the local business markets, spreading the cost of municipal services among a greater number of people, and creating a larger labor pool which might attract business and industry. It would be preferable if suburban communities voluntarily accepted more heterogeneous elements into their population, but, if necessary, this can be imposed. Nathan Glazer, in his article, "Housing Problems and Housing Policies," stated:

> I think we have good social grounds for imposing a certain amount of discomfort on people who would prefer to live in communities of like and like-minded people. We can impose this discomfort when the common desire restricts others' rights to housing; we may impose this discomfort when some large social end dictates a new and different use for the land of the community in which they live.

Suburban areas have often resembled isolated island communities which refused to recognize their relationship to the region in which they are located. Aloofness from regional needs has caused severe problems for our cities and certain elements of the population; this can no longer be tolerated. Twentieth-century America is an urban nation with a diversified social, racial, and economic population, and suburbia must reflect the society of which it is part.

BIBLIOGRAPHY

ONE OF THE EARLIEST, most readable and most widely read exposés on exclusionary zoning was in the New York *Times Magazine*, November 7, 1971, in an article entitled, "The Suburbs Have to Open Their Gates" by Linda and Paul Davidoff and Neil N. Gold. This article and others based much of their statistical and evidentiary support for the widespread existence of exclusionary zoning on the thorough documentation of housing and land-use practices found in the reports from the National Commission on Urban Problems,

"Building the American City" and the President's Committee on Urban Housing, "A Decent Home," published in 1968 and 1969, respectively.

More recently, two reports have provided detailed evaluations of the impact of various housing developments and policies. "The Costs of Sprawl" prepared by the Real Estate Research Corporation in 1974 for the Council on Environmental Quality, the Department of Housing and Urban Development and the Environmental Protection Agency explored the economic and environmental effects of various development patterns and housing types. "Housing and Suburbs; Fiscal and Social Impact of Multifamily Development," prepared by the New Jersey County and Municipal Government Study Commission in 1974, looks at New Jersey communities and the fiscal impact of multifamily developments in comparison to single-family developments.

Further support is offered for a more rational studied land-use policy in the 1973 report, "The Use of Land: A Citizen's Policy Guide to Urban Growth," edited by William K. Reilly for the Rockefeller Brothers Fund with specific recommendations for planned, large-scale, well-designed residential developments with reduced incentives to practice exclusionary zoning. The report, "Review and Evaluation of Research in the Effects of Land Use Controls and Housing Costs," prepared by the Center for Urban and Regional Studies at the University of North Carolina in 1974 for the National Science Foundation, provided specific recommendations to reduce the effect of development controls and other codes on increased housing costs.

The need to define exclusionary zoning and to describe its various and subtle components has been met in a variety of publications: Paul Davidoff and Neil N. Gold, "Exclusionary Zoning," *Yale Review of Law and Social Action,* I (Winter, 1970); Richard Babcock and Fred Bosselman, *Exclusionary Zoning, Land Use Regulation and Housing in the 1970s* (New York, 1973), and Mary E. Brooks, "Exclusionary Zoning" (American Society of Planning Officials, 1970).

Many specific studies of the nature of exclusionary zoning have been prepared; some of the more available ones are: Pennsylvania State Department of Community Affairs, "A Study of Exclusion" (prepared by the Suburban Action Institute), 1973; Urban Research Center, Hunter College of the City University of New York, "The Relationship of Zoning to Housing Adequacy and Availability for Those of Low and Moderate Incomes," July 1968; Suburban Action Institute, "Open or Closed Suburbs: Corporate Location and the Urban Crisis," 1971; National Committee Against Discrimination in Housing, "Jobs and Housing," March 1971; The Regional Plan Association, "Linking Skills, Jobs, and Housing in the New York Region," March, 1972; Morton Lustig, "Standards for Housing in Suburban Communities Based Upon Zoning for Work" (Government Study Center, University of Pennsylvania), 1972; Plainfield, N.J., Planning Division, "Suburban Zoning Practices Surrounding Plainfield," January, 1971; and Westchester County, N.Y., Department of Planning, "Zoning Ordinances and Administration," June, 1970.

References on the legal questions involved in exclusionary zoning issues are indeed numerous. Two of the earliest and most comprehensive explorations into these issues are: Lawrence G. Sager, "Exclusionary Zoning: Constitutional Limitations on the Power of Municipalities to Restrict the Use of Land," American Civil Liberties Union, 1972; and Norman Williams, Jr., and Thomas Norman, "Exclusionary Land Use Controls: The Case of Northeastern New Jersey," *Syracuse Law Review*, 22 (1971). A more recent publication discussing the landmark decision in *Southern Burlington County NAACP* v. *Township of Mount Laurel* has been prepared by the American Society of Planning Officials in a special issue of the *Land Use Law and Zoning Digest*, 27, No. 6 (1975). For further legal references, the reader is directed to the bibliographies listed below.

Several publications have focused on the need for inclusionary zoning to take place to erase the effects of past discrimination and exclusionary zoning and in recognition of the need for affirmative action to achieve equal opportunities. One of the earliest, which in fact coined the phrase "inclusionary zoning," was prepared by Paul and Linda Davidoff in 1971 entitled, "Open the Suburbs: Toward Inclusionary Land Use Controls," *Syracuse Law Review*, 22 (1971). Later publications are: Mary E. Brooks, "Lower Income Housing: The Planners Response" (American Society of Planning Officials, 1972); Anthony Downs, *Opening Up the Suburbs: An Urban Strategy for America* (New Haven, 1973); Leonard S. Rubinowitz, *Low-Income Housing: Suburban Strategies* (Cambridge, 1974); and Herbert M. Franklin, David Falk, and Arthur Levin, "In-Zoning—A Guide for Policy-Makers on Inclusionary Land Use Programs" (The Potomac Institute, 1974).

Two important bibliographies are available which are recent and quite thorough. One is contained in the reference cited above, "In-Zoning—A Guide for Policy-Makers on Inclusionary Land Use Programs," and the other was prepared by the National Committee Against Discrimination in Housing and the Urban Land Institute, entitled, "Fair Housing and Exclusionary Land Use," 1974, which also contains a useful summary of relevant court cases and other actions to encourage low- and moderate-income housing.

CITIES AND SUBURBS IN EUROPE AND THE UNITED STATES
by Frank J. Coppa

MANKIND HAS FORMED CITIES of one kind or another for thousands of years. Civilization originated in the city and to a large degree remains centered there. The cities of the world have played an important role in shaping the course of human history and providing man with his high standard of living and rising expectations. Nonetheless, before the industrial revolution, cities contained only a small part of the total population. As late as 1800 only 3 per cent of the world lived in centers of 5,000 or more; today such centers contain more than 50 per cent of the world's people with over half the population of North America and one third the population of Europe living in cities of at least 100,000. Thus in the last century and a half the world has approached an urbanized state.

The continued attraction of urban life and the movement from the countryside to the city has helped to spark another migration, this one from the city to its periphery. City and suburb are the opposite sides of the same coin so that the fortune of one influences the fate of the other. In the United States a combination of unfortunate circumstances including racial tensions, the widespread use of the automobile, prodigious waste, and unwise governmental policy have contributed to the centrifugal movement and the flight to the urban fringe. Across the Atlantic the cities of the Continent have shown a remarkable vitality and continue to attract to their core not only their own nationals but visitors from all over the world. Why have so many European cities prospered while city after city in the United States succumbed to blight and decay?

In part the well-being of the European city is due to the prevailing notion on the Continent that civilization and urbanity are urban accomplishments. The amenities of life, it is felt, can only be found in the urban areas which contain the great theaters, opera houses, music halls, libraries, universities, museums, sports stadiums, zoos, and churches. European cities are not only the centers of finance, the home of publishers of books, newspapers, and periodicals, the locus of the countries' roads, railways, and air routes but the very barometers of their national wealth and importance. Far older than our own for the most part, European towns, even those with an ancient past, are better preserved because they are more appreciated. While many of these cities have suburbs, and have had them for hundreds of years, they are not generally encircled by suburban sprawl in the American sense.

This essay will examine the conditions that have enabled Europeans to protect their urban centers, many of which were destroyed in the world wars and laboriously rebuilt, while we have allowed ours, untouched by two world conflagrations, to deteriorate. It will dwell upon those centripetal forces on the Continent which have restrained the frenzied rush to the periphery and prevented a duplication of the suburbanization found in the United States.

Suburbs, the outer part of a continuously built-up city and not separated from it by intervening land, have been in existence for thousands of years. Such regions were to be found about the ancient city-states of Sumeria and Greece and about Imperial Rome. Medieval Florence and Venice spawned suburbs as did London by the sixteenth century. In France a royal decree of 1724 concluded that Paris had become too large and established a new boundary line, prohibiting construction in the suburbs beyond. More recently, suburbs have become a common feature of European and

American towns of the nineteenth and twentieth centuries. Where they housed only dwellings and merchants serving the local inhabitants, they were dubbed residential or dormitory suburbs while those containing widespread productive capacity were christened industrial suburbs.

The suburbs of the concentrated European city or the United States of the nineteenth and early twentieth century are quite different from the overspill from American urban areas occurring in the last three decades. This is a unique type of development which tends to be the preserve of the more fortunate members of American society. Indeed some have suggested that this latest settlement be termed the North American pattern to differentiate it from the traditional suburbs of the past which were Old World in origin.

Whether one refers to the new development as the North American pattern, suburbanization, or suburban sprawl, it originated in the United States and is still far more common here than in Europe. Such sprawl consists of a real ring of settlement about the city, it enjoys a lower density of population than the city it surrounds and its population density tends to decrease the further one moves from the core.

A circular settlement of this type, as in the case of the "foot and hoof" city, depends upon individual transportation. In the walking city the limits of human and animal power assured the compactness of the settlement. The railroad and later the tram enabled men to commute for longer distances, but the technology of these modes of public transport hindered continuous habitation. Rather it encouraged clusters of concentration which corresponded to the various railway stops, interspersed by open land. Only when the widespread use of the automobile suddenly revitalized individual transportation was there reproduced the circular city, but on a far vaster scale. Hence suburbanization or universal sprawl is in many ways the child of the automobile and the superhighway.

The massive spread of urban development beyond the boundaries of the city has given rise to yet another term, the metropolitan region which encompasses an enormous geographical extent. The simultaneous growth of several of such metropolitan cities within a small radius often caused them to merge into the polynuclear metropolis or what Patrick Geddes has termed "conurbation," the growing together of several important, independent cities. This has already occurred in places such as the English midlands, the Rhine-Ruhr area of Germany, and in the northeastern region of the United States from Washington to Boston, sometimes called megalopolis.

Recent studies have shown that the daily commuting between the major metropolitan centers in such conurbations is insignificant, but that commuting in the various metropolitan regions is very high. Apparently most suburbs in the United States still depend upon their inner cities which continue to house those functions which serve the entire area. Despite this economic interdependence, the metropolis all too often lacks the power and authority to determine the course of events within its confines. The perpetuation of local government segments the region and often contributes to the deterioration of the core. To make matters worse, many who live in the suburbs are escapist, no longer aware of any responsibility to the area they have abandoned. These are only a few of the problems that have plagued American cities in the post-World War II period.

The migration of the poor and dispossessed into the cities of the United States without control or federal supervision contributed to the crowding and high crime rate in the nation's center cities. While those most in need of assistance poured in, many who were capable of funding the services required hastily left, creating a revolving-door syndrome. The retreat to fortress suburbia was not only prompted by the lure of space, the prospect of home ownership, and the promise of better schools but also the changing class structure of the city and the fear of racial confrontation and violence. The consequences were disastrous for the urban core as in city after city a white minority and a black majority were left behind to cope with the pressing problems of crime, drug addiction, slum housing, rising welfare costs, and staggering property taxes.

While many European cities witnessed a movement to
suburbia and even exurbia, in none did it assume the nature
of a flight. There are many reasons for this divergence. European urban centers are of a wide variety of types. The cities
of "inner" Europe, the industrial heartland of the Continent,
differ substantially from those of "outer" Europe, which remains rural and agricultural. Throughout, commercial and industrial centers exist by the side of political and administrative
centers. Nationality and language provide another means of
differentiation and some have seen important contrasts between the cities of Latin and Germanic Europe.

Despite these differences, many European cities share features which serve to separate them from their American
counterparts. The atmosphere of a city, it has been argued, is
determined by the specific historical conditions under which it
adjusted to rapid expansion. Since many American towns
achieved the rank of major urban centers during an industrial
and commercial age, they sometimes emphasized business
needs at the expense of the human element. Many of the
cities of Europe, on the other hand, adjusted to economic
transformation more gradually, often influenced by aristo-
cratic values as much as utilitarian needs. This is reflected in
Vienna, Paris, Rome, and Madrid and countless smaller
towns whose ambience mirrors an appreciation of the aesthetic and the idealization of leisure as much as efficiency and
the profit motive.

Since many of the cities of Europe are older than the central governments to which they now offer allegiance—some
have a Greek, Roman, Medieval, Baroque, as well as an early
modern past—they have a far stronger tradition of autonomy
and independence than most American cities which are the
creatures of the various states. In addition, European cities
have a long history of regulating and subordinating private
activity for the welfare of the collectivity, refusing to bow to
the *laissez-faire* notions which became virtual dogma in the
United States and England.

The greater control European cities have over their own
affairs and destinies, among other things, leads to the sharp

differentiation between urban and rural areas found in Europe. It also helps to explain why the European cities, most of which are older than the American ones, do not display the same degree of deterioration and decay. Indeed if one were not familiar with the two world wars, whose major battles were fought in Europe, one might conclude that it was the cities of the United States that were bombed and overrun, judging from the many areas that are burned and abandoned.

Psychological as well as physical factors account for the absence in Europe of the massive deterioration characteristic of scores of cities in the wealthiest country in the world. In part, this flows from the fact that there is less antiurbanism in the Old World than the New. This is not to deny that some European thinkers sought relief from the hustle and bustle of city life and like Horace praised life in the country free from jostling crowds, burdensome social obligations, and political intrigue. Indeed before the impact of industrialization transformed social relations Jean Jacques Rousseau denounced luxury and sophistication and called for a return to simplicity and nature. The Romantic Movement which ensued in the nineteenth century also criticized artificial city life but found itself confronted with an older classical culture which appreciated unity, balance, order, and rationality, finding these qualities not in the simple and spontaneous rural elements but in the cultured and educated city man.

From the first, Americans identified cities with the Europeans and there were those who turned from them in revulsion, insisting that cultural and intellectual independence were necessary to assure the newly achieved political independence. Some of the most influential Americans praised rural life, convinced that their most cherished values could best flourish in such an environment. Thomas Jefferson was not alone in his view that large cities were foreign and detrimental to the health, morals, and liberty of Americans. Emerson, Thoreau, and other American writers looked askance at the city. In the eighteenth and the first half of the nineteenth century the yeoman farmer, who supposedly lived a simple, unspoiled life, remained the national ideal.

In the works of Frederick Jackson Turner, perhaps the figure who has influenced the writing and teaching of American history most, the frontier with its open space and vast resources was the crucible which differentiated the American from his European cousins, providing him with a spirit of self-reliance and love of freedom uniquely American. Presenting these ideas first in an essay of 1893, "The Significance of the Frontier in American History," he elaborated upon the importance of the frontier in a series of other works including his *The Rise of the New West* and *The Significance of Sections in American History*.

Antiurbanism was often intertwined with nativism in the United States. City life was denounced as effete and corrupt and urban centers were seen as citadels of crime, sin, political bosses, and strange immigrants. In the second half of the nineteenth century when the country became increasingly urbanized, many Americans did not appreciate this development and held it responsible for the decline of man's communal nature and the growing social dislocation and unhappiness.

State legislatures, controlled by rural constituencies, enacted laws which discriminated against the growing urban centers often not hiding their belief that those centers were necessary for defense and manufacture but they were alien and therefore dangerous. Such thoughts have become deeply implanted in the national psyche so that even though the United States is a nation of cities, Americans are not truly an urban people for their ideal culture remains nonurban. This is reflected in the sad state of American cities.

Interestingly enough the systematic study of cities in the United States was initiated by individuals who were in the main born and raised in nonurban environments. Small wonder that so many of them found the cities chaotic. Often the reforms they suggested were more attuned to the small towns from which they came than the complex cities they sought to improve. The attempts to preserve features of small town life under radically different circumstances has contributed to the animosity against centralized metropolitan government in favor of limited and fragmented local government, as seen in the determination to preserve the political autonomy of the suburban sectors of the various metropolitan regions.

For the European, free of the "Currier and Ives" illusion of rural life and acutely aware that the city assures security, education, prosperity, in short, the better life, the ideal remains to live in the city and there is a tendency to mock the provincial people who have not the good sense or the means to be able to do so. Cities continue to exert a magnetic attraction for the European because their density of population provides the opportunity for specialization and self-realization unattainable elsewhere.

At the same time most urbanites in Europe do not equate mobility with success as do so many Americans who have no appreciation of dwelling for generations in the same neighborhood, perhaps the same house. To mobile Americans, programed to move into bigger if not better houses, this would be tantamount to stagnation. To the European it is stability, and it offers the solace of living and dying among relatives and friends in the place one was born rather than being surrounded by strangers in a more prestigious area. When a man spends his entire life in one neighborhood he develops a far deeper attachment to his community and has a greater stake in its preservation. This situation, multiplied many times, helps to account for the care Europeans lavish upon their cities.

Americans in comparison have nomadic traits. In the United States the population is so mobile that one family in five moves every year. Few live where they were born and a family changes residence many times in a generation. Given this situation the European notion of the city as a stable community does not apply in the New World. The sense of allegiance to the local community is slight. Thus the abandonment of the central cities is not a unique development and was preceded in the United States by the mass exodus from the countryside and there may well be a movement out of suburbia someday.

It might be argued that the European stress on stability rather than mobility reflects the fact that they generally have far fewer opportunities than Americans, and this is unquestionably the case. The endlessly sprawling American suburb is perhaps the most wasteful settlement ever devised. It could only multiply to such proportions in the United States which contains less than 6 per cent of the world's population but annually consumes over 35 per cent of its nonrenewable resources. Even after the economic miracle of the post-World War II period, Europeans remain less wealthy than Americans and must take greater care in preserving what they have. They cannot afford to neglect or abandon their homes or apartments because the prospect of acquiring another is very slim. This provides another incentive to maintain their neighborhoods and cities.

In Europe when there are opportunities for movement and advancement the decision to leave one area for another is generally made by the father. The Continental family is not yet child-oriented or child-dominated and it does not permit the youngest and least capable to determine its future. The head of the family will often refuse to commute long distances simply to provide the children with more room while the mother carefully weighs the social isolation of such a step. European practicality favors employment near home so the worker can leave his job for a few hours and return to his home for lunch and a midafternoon nap. Certain cities of Europe, in fact, come to a virtual standstill between twelve and three to resume their hectic pace only after the midday respite.

European parents who consider their own needs first are not acting to harm their children, for their cities are more people-oriented than American cities with parks and public places which provide areas for relaxation and recreation. These centers also cater to the needs of the aged and the infirm who are not shunned by the population at large nor victimized by roving bands of young delinquents. They are not segregated into nursing homes to be abused, for European culture, unlike our own, respects age and has not yet succumbed to the cult of youth, money, and mobility.

Physical as well as psychological and legal factors contribute to the preservation of the cities of Europe to which Americans and other tourists flock each year. These centers have survived better because they are constructed of more durable material, and built to last rather than merely impress. Maintenance is guaranteed by the government which closely regulates the upkeep of residential as well as commercial buildings. The fact that European apartments are often purchased rather than rented also helps to account for the excellent maintenance in comparison to the deterioration found in many cities. Finally most European cities have not been torn by racial strife as have those in the United States.

Americans, critical of the more rigid class divisions in Europe, are very conscious of both class and color and on both accounts have discriminated against Negroes and other racial minorities. What aggravated the situation was the new mobility and militancy of blacks after World War II. In the two decades after 1940, the greater part of the agricultural population of the Mississippi Delta left the farms as a result of mechanization. The dislocated population of the southern states streamed north sending millions of blacks to the big cities of the North and West, especially Chicago, New York, Detroit, Washington, D.C., and Los Angeles.

In 1940 more than half of all American Negroes lived in rural areas but by 1970 three out of every five blacks lived in the central city of a major metropolitan area according to the Bureau of the Census. This influx of poor blacks disturbed a good part of the urban upper and middle classes and played a part in their exodus from the inner cities. As they abandoned the core, settling on the outskirts, a white suburban collar was constructed about the increasingly black city from Washington to Detroit. Blacks have been excluded from these suburbs by subtle discrimination and overt hostility, the value and type of housing built, and zoning laws.

The racial element in the race to the suburbs in the United States is not repeated in Europe where the population of the various nation-states is far more homogeneous in its racial makeup. There is regional disequilibrium and even the most prosperous and progressive European states have their underdeveloped regions where population often remains well below the national average. Finally economic opportunities vary from country to country and this has sparked a considerable Continental migration. However, the various European governments can put a halt to this movement of workers if their economies warrant such a step. Furthermore many migrants are not permitted to obtain citizenship and can readily be sent home as the Swiss recently threatened to do to their foreign work force.

It is not only the national states that closely control the passage of people across their frontiers, the various cities of the Continent likewise preserve tighter control upon their populations than do American cities. For one thing they rigidly maintain the legal differences between city and countryside. They continue the medieval tradition of cities jealously guarding their rights which they refuse to extend to the surrounding region. There also is a tradition of municipal control over the adjacent countryside, a right which is almost as old as the Greek Polis. Thus many of the cities of Europe have prevented suburban sprawl from spreading further by restricting the use of utilities in the nearby underdeveloped areas. Gas, electrical, sewage and water lines are not permitted to fringe areas without considerable thought and study. In Federal planning law prohibits any new project in that is not directly related to the expansion of France a series of laws employed to strictly control the cities of Europe help to explain why they have not experienced the neglect and mismanagement endured by cities in the United States. The simplicity of the charters of these cities also leads to greater efficiency than found across the Atlantic. In most European cities the Town Council is elected by the residents and all other officials are selected by this body. Consequently, responsibility for policy is readily fixed and this facilitates the redress of grievances. Municipal control, if not ownership, of a series of services such as bus and trolley lines, gas and electrical service, is the established policy in nearly all British and many Continental cities providing yet another mechanism for their autonomy.

The European tax system also works to uphold the influence and independence of their municipalities. In Latin Europe—France, Italy, and Spain the *octroi* or tariff system prevails. Under its provisions a good part of the revenue of the town comes from a customs tax collected on the food and produce which enters the city. Each city is surrounded by a tariff wall as is the state, and this serves not only to separate the city from the surrounding countryside but also to assure its fiscal independence. Property, as such, only pays a small part of the local tax. There are no burdensome property that would serve as an incentive to sell one's ho center city.

The revenue of many Germa
tax which again do
erty in fa

he national average. Finally economic opportunities vary
from country to country and this has sparked a considerable
Continental migration. However, the various European governments can put a halt to this movement of workers if their
economies warrant such a step. Furthermore many migrants
are not permitted to obtain citizenship and can readily be sent
home as the Swiss recently threatened to do to their foreign
work force.

It is not only the national states that closely control the
passage of people across their frontiers, the various cities of
the Continent likewise preserve tighter control upon their
populations than do American cities. For one thing they
rigidly maintain the legal differences between city and countryside. They continue the medieval tradition of cities
zealously guarding their rights which they refuse to extend to
the surrounding region. There also is a tradition of municipal
control over the adjacent countryside, a right which is almost
as old as the Greek Polis. Thus many of the cities of Europe
have prevented suburban sprawl from spreading further by
restricting the use of utilities in the nearby underdeveloped
areas. Gas, electrical, sewage and water lines are not permitted in fringe areas without considerable thought and study. In
Germany, federal planning law prohibits any new project in
the urban fringe that is not directly related to the expansion
of the existing areas, while in France a series of laws em-
power the various levels of government to strictly control
urban sprawl.

Various European cities exercise an extraordinary influence
over their surrounding regions. Amsterdam, for example, can
legislate on all matters of local interest which have not been
regulated by the national government. In Sweden as well as
Great Britain the cities can point to a record of local control
which preceded the emergence of central supervision. Such
British cities as Manchester as well as London have the right
to petition Parliament for a private bill, that is, a law applying
to their area and granting them powers not accorded elsewhere.

The broad political and administrative rights enjoyed by

the cities of Europe help to explain why they have not experienced the neglect and mismanagement endured by cities in the United States. The simplicity of the charters of these cities also leads to greater efficiency than found across the Atlantic. In most European cities the Town Council is elected by the residents and all other officials are selected by this body. Consequently, responsibility for policy is readily fixed and this facilitates the redress of grievances. Municipal control, if not ownership, of a series of services such as bus and trolley lines, gas and electrical service, is the established policy in nearly all British and many Continental cities providing yet another mechanism for their autonomy.

The European tax system also works to uphold the influence and independence of their municipalities. In Latin Europe—France, Italy, and Spain the *octroi* or tariff system prevails. Under its provisions a good part of the revenue of the town comes from a customs tax collected on the food and produce which enters the city. Each city is surrounded by a tariff wall as is the state, and this serves not only to separate the city from the surrounding countryside but also to assure its fiscal independence. Property, as such, only pays a small part of the local tax. There are no burdensome property taxes that would serve as an incentive to sell one's holdings in the center city.

The revenue of many German cities flows from an income tax which again does not encourage the sale of urban property in favor of rural or suburban land. English cities derive revenue from taxes known as rates which are assessed upon the rental value of property and paid by the tenant rather than the owner. Vacant property pays little or no tax so that suburban land which may be worth hundreds of thousands of dollars either pays no tax or it is assessed as a pleasure or hunting preserve. This system provides a premium for keeping suburban land out of use and therefore contributes to the curtailment of suburbanization.

The greater European success in controlling urban overspill is surprising in light of the fact that the population of Western Europe is larger than that of the United States, 253 million in the European Economic Community to 213 million in the United States, while its land area is much smaller, 587,000 square miles to 3,615,000 square miles. This has led to a higher density of population in Europe. It is 359.1 per square mile in France, 639.3 in Italy, 880.3 in Great Britain, 936.4 in Western Germany and 84.9 in the United States.

In the European countries whose population density is four to ten times higher than in the United States, replacing wood and field with brick and asphalt must be carefully considered for land is not only scarce but expensive. Furthermore a considerable portion must be kept in forest in order to protect the environment and prevent floods and erosion. The fact that much of the agricultural land on the outskirts of the various cities is fragmented, as a result of the inheritance system, renders it difficult for capitalists to acquire large tracts for housing developments.

The task of the European builder is further complicated by the fact that many farmers in the Old World do not assume the pragmatic stance of American agriculturists. They are not easily persuaded that they could farm as well elsewhere, displaying a sentimental attachment to the land which is translated into a reluctance to sell even when lured by attractive prices. These problems plus the regulatory control of the town tend to hinder the accumulation of capital for housing and suburban development in Europe.

The shortage of land vis-a-vis population places a premium upon it and contributes to the pressure to control its use in such a manner to assure reserves for agriculture and recreation. The United States with far more land and a greater aversion to control can afford to be more wasteful. Thus the vast geographical extent and wealth of the United States—its gross national product is some 1,050 billion dollars in comparison to 695 billion dollars for the European Economic Community—have created problems for its cities while the shortages found in Europe have proven to be a blessing in disguise.

America's wealth and technology conspired to bring the amenities of urban life to widely scattered suburbs, with the septic tank, electrification, and the automobile playing particularly important roles. Clustering of any kind is directly proportional to the cost and mode of transportation, the lower the cost and the more individual the form, the greater the degree of dispersion. The widespread use of the automobile, combined with cheap petrol and a government-financed system of roads, permitted the modern flight out of the center cities and the flowering of the suburbs. The television and the telephone contributed to remove the sense of isolation. Together with the automobile they made the American suburb, dependent upon space and rapid, individual locomotion, possible.

The use and ownership of automobiles, the single most important factor that permitted modern American suburbanization, was not widespread in Europe until after World War II. Even then far fewer Europeans than Americans could afford to own and maintain one car, let alone the two or sometimes three owned by suburban families in the United States. While the expenditure on personal transportation, that is to say, the automobile, as a percentage of all private consumption was 14.3 per cent in the United States, it was only 8.8 per cent in the United Kingdom, 7.8 per cent in Italy, 7.5 per cent in France and 4.3 per cent in the Netherlands.

In the early 1970s there were some 55 million automobiles registered in the countries of the Common Market while the United States, with its smaller population, had some 110 million. Furthermore while European appreciation of the automobile approached the automania found in the United States, their use of this mode of transportation was rather more limited. The high cost of petrol, almost totally imported, acted as a deterrent to the widespread use of the automobile. Finally the governments of the Western European states were not as extravagant in their roadbuilding as the federal government. Instead, they continued to spend money on mass transit: trains, trolleys, buses, and subways, thus encouraging the concentration rather than the dispersion of population. Presently, researchers in Great Britain, Western Germany, France, and

Italy are experimenting with electric-powered buses and some are already in use.

The impact of transportation upon the clustering of population is apparent in Belgium, a country of ancient towns and vigorous urban industrial development. In the nineteenth century first the state railways followed by private lines offered the working classes cheap rates of travel which by the end of the century extended to one hundred kilometers. As a result the countryside was not depopulated and this policy moderated the rapid expansion of the country's major urban centers as well as curtailed suburbanization. In fact between 1890 and 1910, the size commune, which claimed the largest share of the national population increase, were those of 5,000 to 25,000 souls, a feat which continued in the post-World War II period. This trend was in large measure the result of the government's railroad policy which discouraged the enormous expansion of urban centers into their adjacent countryside and encouraged the development of residential areas some distance away from the main centers of employment.

Not all Europeans have been as fortunate as the Belgians in their attempts to control the size of their cities and check suburban sprawl. The English have long been distressed by the extraordinary growth of the London area to the point where it accounts for some 23 per cent of the total population of England to the detriment of Scotland, Wales, the Northeast, and the Northwest. At the turn of the century Ebenezer Howard shared the aversion to huge metropolitan centers and in his book, *Garden Cities of Tomorrow* (1898), called for an alternative. He felt that the continued growth of cities such as London, Paris, and Berlin had not produced any gains in social life and threatened to prove detrimental to the national well-being.

Howard's garden city, a town that is sufficiently large to make possible a full measure of social life but not so large as to lead to alienation and anomie, was surrounded by a rural belt. This garden city of approximately 32,000 souls sought at once to relieve the congestion of the great city without urban overspill degenerating into suburbanization. Suburban areas, because they lacked an industrial population and a working base, he considered one of the most artificial environments ever created by man. Thus his vision of the garden city did not provide for a grouping of individual residences with immense spaces between them but a confined urban center which would provide homes for 30,000 people on one thousand acres. The permanent belt of open agricultural land was used to limit the spread of the city from within while preventing encroachments from outside.

In 1903 a corporation was organized to implement Howard's ideas, establishing Letchworth, thirty-four miles northwest of London. Partly inspired by his concept, the British Parliament in 1938 passed the Green Belt Act which limited the extension of London by creating a five-mile-wide girdle of permanent open countryside about the sprawling metropolitan area. The government also restricted the flow of traffic into the center so that only some 8 per cent of those who enter the core do so by automobile. Complementing this restrictive approach, the British planned for a series of satellite cities beyond the country belt to accommodate the overspill from London. To prevent people from commuting across the cordon into London, the new towns were to be self-contained, providing sufficient employment for those who moved there.

In 1943 the Ministry of Town and Country Planning was created with jurisdiction over local government as well as land utilization. While the Greater London Plan of 1944 concentrated upon the building of new towns outside the belt, the Town Development Act of 1952 sought to relieve congestion not by the creation of such new centers but by the enlargement of the existing ones. British planners, painfully aware that they had not succeeded in decongesting London by means of their new towns, sought other solutions, and looked to the remaining large cities of southeastern England such as Portsmouth and Southampton to take some of the pressure off greater London.

Ebenezer Howard's ideas influenced the planning of Hilversum in the Netherlands and Ernest May's satellite communities in Frankfurt and found strong adherents and admirers in

France, who agreed with Howard that the size of towns is a proper subject of conscious control. Recently the President of France, Valéry Giscard d'Estaing, announced plans for the establishment of a vast green belt around Paris which would include the plains of the Ile de France and Versailles to the north and west of the city and the plateaus in the south and east. A number of Americans also have advocated planned communities and controlled urban growth. However, for the most part they have been frustrated by a lack of national commitment to such ideas and the authority to translate planning into action.

In contrast, Europe has a long tradition of planned urban growth. Paris was the first great capital to be planned following the ambitious designs outlined by the Academy of Architects for the Sun King, Louis XIV. The royal roads were built to radiate from Notre Dame de Paris which remains the reference point for measuring distances. The transfer of the capital from Paris to Versailles in the seventeenth century did not curtail the city's growth or influence. Later, in the nineteenth century, Napoleon Bonaparte sought to transform Paris into a city worthy to be called his capital, and his nephew, Napoleon III, continued the expansion and beautification of the city in line with his imperial ambitions. A good part of the railway construction undertaken during the Second Empire (1852–70) favored the capital, for priority was given to lines emanating from Paris.

These endeavors helped to make possible the domination of the capital, which is considered avant-garde, over the rest of the country, which is considered backward in comparison. This domination is quantitative as well as qualitative. In the century from 1860 to 1960, while the population of France grew by less than 20 per cent, the population of Paris virtually tripled so that today the metropolitan area accounts for almost 20 per cent of the national total on less than 2 per cent of the country's surface. Indeed the sprawl of the Paris agglomeration has much in common with the suburbanization found about large cities in the United States.

Determined to control the growth of the capital the French

have approved a series of laws to foster the development of regional cities in harmony with the view of the French geographer, Pierre George, that while in the past regions made cities, at present it is the city which determines the nature of the region. It has been suggested that urban centers one hundred to two hundred kilometers from Paris proper be favored in order to regulate the expansion of the capital. The cities which would be enlarged include Orléans, Rouen, Amiens, Troyes, and Chartres.

Some fifteen years ago the French uncovered a master plan for the future of the Paris area which aimed to reduce congestion in the historic core by altering and improving transportation and introducing provisions to prevent obsolescence in the inner city. The current President, Giscard d'Estaing, attaches great importance to the existence of "green spaces" within the capital and restricting the suffocating proliferation of automobiles. As a result he has vetoed a long-planned expressway on the left bank of the Seine River and has decided that the site of the former food market, Les Halles, should be occupied by a park rather than an international commercial center.

Germany, which has a long and important urban tradition, developed city planning into an organized art and from there it spread to the rest of the world. Zoning, the power to control the use of land and the size of buildings, is also of German origin. A number of factors have spurred the Germans to continue their urban planning including the postwar division of Germany, the flood of refugees to the cities of the West, and the destruction of the core of most German cities in the Second World War which necessitated their reconstruction and in some cases led to widespread reorganization.

Urbanization in the Rhine-Ruhr conurbation, which has the greatest population concentration on the European continent, also called for study. This area, which embraces seven metropolitan regions, has a combined population of some 11 million and accounts for 20 per cent of the total population of the Republic. To prevent this conurbation from spreading and absorbing acres needed for agriculture and recreation, green belts have been established between the various cities in the area and their preservation rigidly enforced.

Italy, plagued by a north-south differential, has also sought to curb sprawl. Although it industrialized relatively late, at the end of the nineteenth and the beginning of the twentieth century, the population was fertile and pressed hard upon its geographical base. Its cities, having a tradition of autonomy and long the center of national life, expanded in the post-unification period. Today the majority of Italians live in towns with populations of more than 20,000, but the greatest expansion in urban settlement has been in towns which contain over 100,000 inhabitants. Not only did industrial and commercial towns such as Milan, Genoa, and Turin in the northern industrial triangle prosper and grow, but political and administrative centers such as Rome also mushroomed.

During the age of Giolitti, 1901–14, the capital again needed more room and impinged upon its outlying areas. There were those who wanted to capitalize on the city's need for land hoping to assure themselves windfall profits by purchasing suburban land about Rome. Prime Minister Giovanni Giolitti, who held the Ministry of the Interior as well, proposed legislation for the expansion of the capital and would not allow either the municipality or the national government to be blackmailed. He obtained the peripheral land for Rome at a reasonable price by threatening to expropriate the land, compensating the owners at the rate the land was assessed for taxation.

Despite the municipal expansion this permitted, the population of the city continued to grow and pressed upon the available land, creating a severe housing shortage in the city. The poorer and newer residents of Rome, unable to find adequate housing in the city at a price they could afford, settled in shanties on the outskirts, creating a ring of poverty about the city. Even the authoritarian Fascist regime, which employed a series of expedients to minimize internal migration, found that it could not easily solve the problems of Rome.

In 1939 when the capital was chosen as the seat of a world exhibition to be held in 1942, Mussolini attempted to combine work for the exhibition with the need for municipal expansion. The government decided that the grandiose facilities of the exhibition, designed to show all the power and might of Fascist Italy, should be utilized to provide the foundation and framework of a new and separate quarter of Rome. A site was chosen between Rome and the seacoast, broad streets were laid out, and construction on a number of buildings commenced. A subway was planned to tie the area to the center of Rome. Unfortunately, the project was frustrated by the outbreak of the Second World War.

After the conflict, which only aggravated the urban housing shortage, attention was once again directed to the exhibition area. It offered possibilities for expansion, but initially it was difficult to draw the urban-minded Romans to this location. The opening of the subway persuaded many to make the move and today this area is a sort of model quarter made possible by the co-operation of the central government and the Roman municipality. Thus Rome, like many other European cities, has studied the problem of sprawl and sought to mitigate its effect. Its success has not been complete, for Italians as well as Germans have complained that their cities are being Americanized by suburbanization and the automobile culture, which prizes motels and supermarkets more than social intercourse and the humane civilization found in the historic cities.

The European urban ambience was threatened to some degree by the affluence which resulted from the postwar economic miracle. There are indications that this new economic well-being has encouraged Europeans to imitate the wasteful American system of land use. Furthermore the industrial regeneration has in large measure been based upon the automobile industry so that one worker out of seven in England and Germany depends upon it for his livelihood while one worker out of ten does so in France and Italy. Recently the number of cars in use has grown more rapidly in Britain, France, and Italy than in the United States. Since there are more cars than ever in European hands, some observers feared that the automobile would consume petrol and land as voraciously in

Europe as it has in the United States. Europeans have already commenced building superhighways on a grand scale as can be seen by the magnificent new autobahns of Germany and the autostrade of Italy which total some 10,000 kilometers. There is even talk of a Milan to Moscow superhighway in this new automobile age in Europe.

Despite these developments, a number of considerations are constraining the Europeans to avoid wasteful sprawl and very likely will induce Americans to curtail it as well. Tension in the Middle East and the related increase in the price of imported petroleum has adversely affected the economy of the Western world which already was staggering under the impact of a phenomenal inflation and has even shaken the confidence of citizens of the industrial giant of North America.

If the United States, which still produces some 90 per cent of its own energy is vulnerable, the Europeans, almost totally dependent upon expensive Arab oil, have had their economies, and not just their confidence, shaken. To make matters worse, Europeans had experienced a phenomenal increase of their per capita consumption of energy from 1951 to 1968 going from 810 to 2,129 kilograms in Italy, 2,340 to 3,093 kilograms in France, 2,780 to 4,199 in West Germany, and 4,650 to 5,003 kilograms in the United Kingdom. Even financially stable states have been adversely affected by the increases in the price of crude oil which skyrocketed from $1.80 a barrel in the decade from 1960 to 1970 to $11.25 in 1975. Foreign oil has been a major contributor to the chronic trade deficits of Great Britain as well as Italy and endangers the prosperity of West Germany and the United States as well. While Americans complain that the retail price of a gallon of regular gasoline has climbed to 59.9¢, it has soared to $1.25 in Britain, $1.27 in West Germany, $1.32 in France, and even higher in Italy.

The explosion of oil prices which has led to deficits and balance of payment problems has had its positive side as the various European states have taken steps to curtail the consumption of gasoline, restrict the use of the automobile, and improve public transit. Thus while rail service seems to have screeched to a halt in parts of the United States, it has forged ahead in Western Europe which has introduced a number of new trains and faster, more efficient service. As a result European lines recorded increased passenger usage in 1974, up more than 4 per cent in France and Austria and more than 8 per cent in the Netherlands.

European cities also have begun to react to the problems posed by the automobile by creating auto-free enclaves to preserve their more leisurely way of life and reassert the priority of man over machine. Parisians, choked by more than two million automobiles which compete for insufficient parking spaces, have been encouraged to use the Metro and buses. The French are currently considering banning cars from their central cities as well as imposing tolls, higher automobile registration and parking fees. In downtown Rome, alone, almost five hundred acres have been turned into pedestrian malls.

In fact, Rome recently prohibited the use of the automobile in a fourth section of its historic core in an attempt to stop the strangulation of its narrow twisting streets by bumper-to-bumper traffic and permit Romans to enjoy their coffee at outdoor cafés without the noise and pollution that rendered relaxation impossible. The municipality has been aided by the sale of a monthly pass at a reasonable price which provides for unlimited bus use. This has led to a 40 per cent increase in the use of public transit. Despite the depressed Italian fiscal situation, the government has promised to complete the expensive 14.4-mile subway in the Eternal City.

In Bologna, cars have been banned from the center and in return the municipality has allowed residents to ride some city buses gratis. Florence, Venice, and a number of cities of Northern Europe also have historical sites and an older way of life they wish to protect from the automobile. In the center of the North German city of Cologne, 90 per cent of which was destroyed in the Second World War and rebuilt afterward, the automobile has been confined to a lower level creating a downtown paradise for pedestrians. Unlike Americans, Europeans have not feared government intervention to protect the rights of the citizenry, well aware that without law liberty turns to license.

The energy shortage and the high cost of petrol have reversed some unfortunate tendencies and helped convince Europeans to remain in their urban areas or those suburban communities served by rail where they can rely upon the subways, buses, and trolleys, some of which they imported from the United States. They are fortunate that their urban ambience still permits them to walk to grocery stores and neighborhood butcher shops, community schools, and local houses of worship. Once again the urban tradition has served the European well, enabling him to better cope with a crisis situation. The United States, far more wealthy and less threatened by the oil shortage, would do well to examine the European experience and perhaps consider the cost and consequences of its suburbanization.

BIBLIOGRAPHY

DEAN S. RUGG's *Spatial Foundations of Urbanism* (Dubuque, Iowa, 1972) utilizes a series of geographical concepts to examine urban development and its regional impact. The author has spent many years in Europe and his research in Great Britain, Germany, and Austria provides insight into the comparative aspects of urbanism and suburbanization. Indeed the most original chapters in this work reflect this comparative approach. The pages which concentrate upon spatial elements in the history of urbanism provide a brief historical sketch of urbanization in Europe from the ancient world to the development of suburban sprawl and conurbations. Graphs, charts, maps, and diagrams provide a wealth of information. Elsewhere the author examines the preindustrial city, the Western European city as well as the socialist city, delving both into their external relations and internal features. His description of the distinctive characteristics of the modern Western European city and his analysis of the factors affecting its development are excellent and provide facts and material not readily available elsewhere.

Robert E. Dickinson's *City and Region: A Geographical Interpretation* (London, 1964) also stresses the geographical structure of society and suggests that it is upon the knowledge of the spatial anatomy of an area that planning, including urban-suburban reorganization must be based. Particularly useful is the section on town-country relations, which examines developments in Germany, France, the United States, and England, and the series of chapters on city and region in the United States, Western Europe, and Britain. The concluding chapter examines the international aspects of regionalism.

Ebenezer Howard's *Garden Cities of Tomorrow* (London, 1944), first published at the end of the nineteenth century, is a classic work which holds a unique place in town-planning literature. It inspired the garden-city movement which has found adherents throughout the world and has put forward ideas which have altered our perception of urban evolution. While this work was a reflection of the English ambience its message was almost universally received. Lloyd Rodwin's *Nations and Cities: A Comparison of Strategies for Urban Growth* (Boston, 1970) examines the problem of imbalanced urban development from an international perspective. It enumerates the growth options and some of the techniques employed world wide to restrict the size of metropolitan regions. While the chapter on the United States concentrates upon the quest to save the central city, those on England and France dwell upon the mechanisms utilized by these two states to curtail the growth of their capital cities.

Niles Hansen's *French Regional Planning* (Bloomington, 1968) on the other hand is less broad and delves into the comprehensive national system of regional planning which has evolved in France during the last two decades, stressing the implications of this experience for the United States. The section on the capital is particularly useful for an understanding to the French endeavors to curb, or at least to cope with, the expansion of Paris.

There are innumerable anthologies which examine the

problems flowing from urbanization and suburbanization. Whereas most of these collect the work of specialists of many types including historians, political scientists, economists, and planners, *Metropolis On the Move: Geographers Look at Urban Sprawl* (New York, 1967) is rather different. The contributions in this work, edited by Jean Gottmann and Robert A. Harper, represent the thought of one single type of urban specialist—the geographer. *Cities in Change: Studies on the Urban Condition* (Boston, 1973) is more traditional in its coverage and includes the insights of a wide range of urban scholars. While urbanization and suburbanization are most closely examined in the United States, a number of the articles included in this collection examine the Western European experience.

Likewise, the anthology edited by R. P. Beckinsale and J. M. Houston, *Urbanization and Its Problems* (Oxford, 1968) has a broad scope and includes Africa, Asia, and the Americas. Eight of the essays in this anthology deal solely with parts of Europe, probing such problems as the overspill of modern conurbations in England and Wales, the impact of the railway upon British towns, and the influence of aerial bombardment upon the townscapes of Western Germany. For an in-depth treatment of suburbanization in one country, see the articles edited by Charles M. Haar in *The End of Innocence: A Suburban Reader* (Glenview, Ill., 1972) which consider various aspects of suburbanization in the United States.

THE FUTURE OF THE AMERICAN SUBURBS
by Stanley Buder

THE MODERN SUBURB invariably proves as elusive a concept to define adequately as the middle class who is credited with having created this most recent form of human community in the second half of the last century. In present American usage the term suburb most commonly refers to the areas outside of and proximate to a city's boundaries. But suburb has a specific connotation as well.

Until recently it generally was assumed that the suburbs were composed of residential communities. Providing relatively little employment opportunities, residential communities were directly linked to the city by a variety of critical ties and dependencies. Their subordination was manifested and sustained by a transportation system that radiated outward from the center of the city, creating an umbilical cord which permitted nurture but never total development into a complete community.

Distinct from the small town, which in some ways it otherwise resembled, the residential suburb must be viewed as an expression of important modern changes involving the family. The suburb as we know it today developed during the nineteenth century when the family began to shift from being principally a unit of production to one essentially concerned with consumption—with much of a family's expenses going for the use of the house not only as basic shelter but also as a focus for amenities, status, recreation, and leisure.

The home and its setting as an expression of a life-style divorced from production originated with the affluent and prosperous. In time, however, this concept was absorbed by much of the population, through a process that the British sociologists Young and Willmott have called "Stratified Diffusion." The results of this process are that most American families perceive housing and neighborhoods as keys to their hoped-for style of life, and indices of their status and material success.

Spatial separation of work and residence that occurred in the early nineteenth-century industrial city made possible the bedroom suburb. For this division permitted the middle class to search on an ever-advancing urban periphery for an alternative residential environment to the densely built-up, dirty, and often dangerous older areas of "great cities." Of necessity, however, family breadwinners returned to the city business districts in the daytime to find employment. The modern family of clearly segregated functions was being shaped: The wife's place was in the home, while the husband was expected to provide the wherewithal for a proper home.

In sociological terms, the function of the dormitory suburb was to provide a family-oriented, home-centered environment for the affluent. Here residents created socially homogeneous, status enhancing, and safe communities. A paramount concern was that the communities be attractive. By the end of the nineteenth century this meant rural-like rather than urban appearing. The middle-class residential suburb that has been briefly described above remains important, both as a reality and, perhaps more importantly, as a symbol of family success and aspiration. At present, however, it can no longer be regarded as the prototypical American suburb.

The remarkable rise of suburbs in the decades since World War II has increasingly demanded independent attention apart from their role in urban change and in metropolitan development. Since World War II, American suburbs have altered drastically, entering a second, more complex, and diversified phase. Already by 1970 more Americans dwelled in the metropolitan area outside the city than resided within the latter. Even more suggestive of future change was the economic growth experienced by suburbs. In 1960 they contained only five jobs for every seven in central cities, yet ten years later they had drawn even. The next decades will in all probability experience a further significant outward drift of employment.

Thus the suburbs are now as much a place to work as to live. Traditional dependencies upon the central city are loosening. The ubiquitous automobile and the new rapid expressways built circumferentially around the city since World War II have freed the suburb from its earlier central-city-oriented transportation system. Already the great department stores located in the urban central business districts (CBD) seek to draw customers from the shopping centers of suburbia rather than the other way around. The umbilical cord has been cut.

Obviously the view of the American suburb as primarily an area of middle-class dormitory communities is no longer adequate. Though this view lingers on in the popular mind as an example of cultural lag, students of metropolitan growth, trying to come to terms with our present reality, now refer to recent changes as the "urbanization of the suburbs," or the development of "spread suburbs."

Suburbanization, a process at least a century old, therefore, has already experienced two phases. Some already anticipate a third. But along with change has been continuity: the suburbs are still perceived as a home-centered, family-oriented environment characterized by low density, the single-family house, social homogeneity, and a nonurban appearance. Yet even these elements are being altered. Essential to a consideration of the future of the suburbs is a series of questions: As our suburbs change in what directions are they moving? Is a new order of communities evolving? And if not, should it?

There are several approaches to predicting the future of the American suburb. The more optimistic is to postulate a set of desirable goals, and to assume over time that these will either

be achieved or approximated. A second approach is to ex-
trapolate the future from an analysis of historic developments
and present trends. A third is to anticipate abrupt and fundamental changes that may be neither desirable nor control-
lable.

In any case, change as it affects community organization is
influenced by too many variables for confident prognostication. One must calculate alterations in demographic characteristics, variances in population size and distribution, shifting
economic trends, and possible technological breakthroughs or
setbacks; all of these in turn must be related to evolving social
values and institutions. An article on the future, then, should
be emphatically prefaced with a caveat. Despite these difficulties, or perhaps because of their challenge, men have always
delighted in forecasting or trying to order the future.

As early as the post-Civil War years, when Americans were
first becoming fully conscious of the massive ingathering of
population into their cities, Frederick Law Olmsted observed
sure signs of a slow suburban "countertide of migration . . .
affecting the more intelligent and more fortunate classes." To
Olmsted, famed landscape architect of Central Park and
spokesman for genteel thought, this development was welcomed. He believed "the most attractive refined and most
soundly wholesome forms of domestic life are found in residential suburbs."

In the late 1860s, Olmsted actualized these notions when
he and his partner, the noted architect Calvert Vaux, designed
Riverside, Illinois, a railroad suburb of Chicago. They used
curvilinear, tree-lined streets to create picturesque winding
roads along the parklike embankment of a river. Houses were
carefully placed in a sylvan environment to enhance their
sense of isolation and family privacy. It would be this ideal,
the picturesque suburb of private homes surrounded by nature (even if this could be provided only by the trompe l'oeil
of the landscape architect) that would dominate the twentieth-century dream of the suburbs. The emphasis on the de-
tachment of the family in a physical sense from community

was an expression of the importance given family privacy and self-sufficiency.

A woman resident of Riverside reported: "It is more pleasant in a small community where people are of similar backgrounds, know manners, and wash themselves." Another resident of a new suburb gave as his reasons for moving there the desire for "safe, attractive, and healthful conditions for my family living" as well as "well-bred children for [my] children to play with and . . . desirable social acquaintances." From its beginning, the modern suburb was the result not only of the middle-class interest in greater space for personal use but also of the desire to spatially separate themselves from the mixed land-use and social heterogeneity of the crowded and dirty cities. The suburb, with its characteristic single-family detached houses, was envisioned as a sanctuary from the pressures of modern industrial life.

Railroad suburbs were, of course, for the prosperous and wealthy. By the 1880s a socialist writer could complain that the rich had exited the city except to work, and that "this modern fashionable suburbanism and exclusiveness is a real grievance to the working class. Had the rich continued to live among the masses, they would with their wealth and influence made our large towns pleasant places to live." But if the rich would not return to the city, perhaps they were right in believing the suburbs a superior environment. By the turn of the century, certain social and housing reformers were interested in the possibility of moving many of the urban poor and working class into suburban homes. In other words, suburbia was seen as the setting for the solution of America's urban problems. Such views of the future were popular at the turn of the last century: an era, like our own, of great technological innovation and social unrest. Perhaps the most interesting and influential examples of this viewpoint were Edward Bellamy's novels: *Looking Backward* (1888) and its sequel *Equality* (1899).

Bellamy's books foretold cities of the year 2000 in which "every home stands in its own inclosure," and "which were only a fraction of their former population." Manhattan Island of the future was described as resembling Central Park with 250,000 people living amidst groves and fountains. A majority of the national population, however, would be living at a distance from cities, while the "telephone and electroscope [television]" allowed them to "enjoy the theater, the concert, and the orator quite as advantageously as the residents of the largest cities."

One of many inspired by Bellamy's vision was a middle-aged London stenographer, Ebenezer Howard. In 1898, Howard published a work that has influenced significantly the development of twentieth-century planning theory and practice. This book is now known by the title of the slightly revised edition of 1902: *Garden Cities of Tomorrow*. Dismissed by most contemporary critics as utopian, it has long since acquired a place as a classic of modern planning.

Howard did not intend to predict the future but to create it. He set out to convince a small group of individuals to organize a new type of human community, a community based on the "marriage of city and country." Here all land would be owned in perpetuity by the community. Limited in size—both in terms of area and population—Howard's garden city provided each family its own house and garden, and offered a variety of employment possibilities all within easy distance of the home. An inviolate green belt, preserved for agricultural and recreational use, would girdle the community, allowing town residents easy access to nature. The garden city was viewed as a response to the stagnation of the countryside and the social conflicts and environmental problems of the "great cities." It would be, in effect, a synthesis of the best features of city and country.

On reaching an optimum population, which Howard thought would be in the range of 30,000 to 60,000, the garden city would cease to grow. Instead, a colony would be created. Several garden cities would be eventually located proximate to each other, each having special facilities. Thus a collaborative network of "social cities" would be created. In time, the "great cities" would shrink in size until they, too, became garden cities.

In 1899, Howard organized an association that did indeed build two new towns in Britain. But Howard's work had a broader significance. He raised the issue: Should cities simply grow outward to absorb the countryside, or would society do better to curtail this growth through forms of organized population dispersal? Howard's answer was to disperse population in communities planned for low density and relative economic and social self-sufficiency that would insure the preservation of open countryside. The possibilities seemed so alluring that Patrick Geddes presciently suggested in 1906 that the most important finding of the previous century had been the discovery by the middle class of a new urban environment, that is, the suburb. This was distinctive from existing cities in being based on the single-family home placed in low-density "countrified" settings. He believed that the challenge to the twentieth century was to extend this beneficial environment to the remainder of the population.

Planned use, controlled growth, and a concept of a unified community were the keynotes for all these men. For instance, later supporters of Howard's concepts such as Raymond Unwin in Britain, and the Americans Henry Wright, Clarence Stein, and Lewis Mumford would argue that housing must be built as an integral part of a community, thought through in advance, both in terms of attractiveness, convenience, and safety and the inclusion of a full range of social services. This concept is now known as "planned unit development" and, along with Howard's various concepts—new towns, green belts, regional organization of communities, and controls on population growth and placement—may very well be ideas whose time has come.

A few aspects of Howard's dream have been partially realized, though not in the planned context he intended. His belief that families should each have their own house and garden, and that communities should be characterized by low density and ample open space are a commonplace of the more attractive, and one might add, expensive, middle-class American suburb. Indeed the visitor to Letchworth and Welwyn, the two English communities built by Howard's movement in the years before and immediately after World War I, would find certain manifest similarities in the street scenes with Scarsdale or Lake Forest. Yet Howard's communities were deliberately intended for all classes of society, and were developed as a purposeful and collaborative effort to achieve a supportive and complete community. The failure to implement this part of Howard's idea exemplifies the problem of those who plan for the future without fully taking the aspirations and cultural factors of the people into consideration. Howard's ideas also ran counter to a legal and political system in America which assumed that community development was largely a matter of market forces and the free-enterprise system. Robert Moses aptly described suburban planning in America as a "collusion between inept politicians and hit-and-run speculators."

The motivating vision in the development of the American suburbs has been, and to an extent remains, that of the family preoccupied with achieving a private environment, and extending the family's personal space both within and without the house. Family territoriality, rather than general use or public need, has been the primary concern. This has led to important consequences in physical design, social composition, life-styles, and recently in increased efforts by the American communities to develop legal stratagems to strengthen the bulwarks of their exclusiveness in defense against the forces of social change that threaten to overwhelm them. The American ideal of suburbia—what I call the vision of the private landscape—has been one of the major reasons for the failure to develop comprehensive planning.

Social planners did not influence suburban growth as much as land developers and speculative builders who more fully understood what Americans wanted and catered to that aspiration. In addition, unexpected developments influenced the suburban landscape. For instance, no one could anticipate the importance of the automobile in opening up the suburbs to the masses while at the same time altering its character: The dreams based on the ideals of the early middle-class suburbs would remain, but a different reality has emerged.

The automobile has influenced the development of the suburb in several ways, though the results have become apparent only in the last decade. To begin with, it encouraged a new sprawl-type pattern of settlement. That allowed—once adequate expressway systems were constructed—suburban tract development on relatively low-cost land within a radius of forty to fifty miles of the city center. The availability of relatively inexpensive houses and lots, based in part on this cheap land and aided by VA and FHA mortgages, permitted large elements in the lower-middle and working class to fulfill the American dream of home ownership in the suburbs. Thus in phase two, as in phase one, the single-family house, in the form of the split level of the fifties and the "ranch" of the sixties, has been the penultimate symbol of suburbia.

The pull of the suburbs on economic activity traditionally associated with the city also was manifested very quickly after World War II. The first to relocate were those manufacturing firms that required large amounts of land in order to organize production horizontally, as in an assembly-line process. But the national superhighway road system started in the Eisenhower years (and the diesel truck) ended the traditional transportation advantages that cities formerly enjoyed as rail and port hubs. By the late 1950s, economists realized that the city had lost out to the suburb in the competition for most forms of manufacturing. Observers noted that during the normal rush-hour traffic, the stream of cars carrying white-collar workers into the CBD was matched by a parallel stream of automobiles conveying blue-collar workers to factory jobs in the suburbs, often located in newly created industrial parks.

It was generally assumed until the late 1960s, however, that the cities would retain a near monopoly on corporate headquarters as well as large banks, insurance firms, and law firms. It is now evident that suburbia is attracting many of these. Aside from economic considerations, many firms relocated in the suburbs for the cachet of offices built on the model of a college campus and also, in some cases, to avoid hiring minority workers who are present in large numbers in the urban work force. The suburbs now have a full range of economic opportunities. The commuter to the city is no longer representative of the suburbanite. And suburbia is no longer a bedroom suburb; it is now a place of production as well as consumption. Not only is there less need for its citizens to go to the city for work, but indeed for any reason besides highly specialized cultural activities.

One beneficial result of this change might be anticipated as a decline in commutation time, and a tendency for people to live and work in the same communities. But this has not really happened. In becoming more diversified, suburban communities have not become complete communities in themselves, as Howard and other planners envisioned. Instead, commuting remains the pattern, but now it is from one suburb to another, or more likely from a suburb to an industrial park, office complex, or shopping mall. In a similar way the wife, too, must look to a variety of widely scattered locations to satisfy the family's needs for professional, commercial, and public services. The need to travel by private automobile, in the absence of effective public transportation systems, to fulfill most important functions is an essential characteristic of our spread suburbs. They lack both the CBD of the great city, and the main street of both the small town and the early twentieth-century suburbs.

The development of suburbia has not fulfilled the social expectations of planners or reformers. The results have been sprawling tract developments often lacking the cores—railroad stations and main streets—that once served to engender some sense of community. Many believe that the new postwar suburbs have not solved the problems of the city but rather exacerbated them. They also have created new problems of their own. In late 1968 a Special Task Force on Suburban Problems reported to President Johnson:

In the rush to provide facilities that so many citizens wanted, suburban land has been cut too fine and built up too thick, and what should have been shapely towns have grown formlessly until the suburban sprawl has destroyed the sense that the citizens could control their own environment. Blight and decay have begun to set in, as they do in any community that has lost the love of its inhabitants. Industry has been moving in, as it should in order to provide jobs near people's homes, but in an unordered and unprepared fashion, resulting in pollution of the air, water, and landscape.

The results of the post-World War II suburban boom clearly show the failure of contemporary planning and the impossibility of simply maintaining the status quo position of earlier suburban life. Unforeseen technological developments plus a fairly healthy economy overwhelmed both and should have alerted us to the need for a more rational method of predicting future events. Yet this was not the case. The dismay over suburban sprawl, compounded with the alarm over conditions in urban areas, led to the dismal predictions of the late 1950s and 1960s. These predictions were based on the perception that an increasing number of families was not simply moving but rather "fleeing" to the suburbs to escape urban blight and the increasing influx of rural blacks moving to the cities of the North.

The factual evidence was even more alarming. In the decades of the 1950s and 1960s, central cities either lost population or remained relatively stable as their suburban populations swelled. But this does not adequately reveal the social transition which occurred in many cities as middle-class whites began to be replaced by newcomers often lacking in education, skills, or capital. At the very time the cities found their tax base eroding and their capital plants aging, they were called upon to provide expensive social services for this new population. A cycle developed: The more problems cities exhibited, the greater the inclination of the remaining middle class to leave, the more serious then became the problems of the cities. In turn, suburbia was becoming the nightmare of urban planners rather than the utopia envisioned by Howard and others a half century before.

Based on a straight-line extrapolation from the past several decades of white flight, some have predicted an ever-worsening condition. They foresee many of our better known cities with drastically reduced populations by the twenty-first century. These, however, would not be the garden cities of Howard's dream but rather crumbling ruins inhabited mostly by those who are economically unable to leave and those blocked from exiting by discrimination—in other words, the poor, the aged, and racial minorities. A "clockwork orange" scenario based on such a possibility was constructed by President Johnson's Commission on Violence in 1967:

> If present trends are not positively redirected by creative new action, we can expect further social fragmentation of the urban environment, formation of excessively parochial communities, greater segregation of different racial groups and economic classes . . . and polarization of attitudes on a variety of issues. It is logical to expect the establishment of the 'defensive city,' the modern counterpart of the fortified medieval city, consisting of an economically declining central business district in the inner city protected by people shopping or working in buildings during daylight hours and 'sealed off' by police during nighttime hours. Highrise apartment buildings and residential 'compounds' will be fortified 'cells' for upper-, middle-, and high-income populations living at prime locations in the inner city. Suburban neighborhoods, geographically removed from the central city, will be 'safe areas,' protected mainly by racial and economic homogeneity and by distance from population groups with the highest propensities to commit crime. Many parts of central cities will witness frequent and widespread crime, perhaps out of police control.

Such a pessimistic view of the future was based on a continuation of existing trends and does not take into account unforeseeable events or technological breakthroughs which might alter the future as they did the past. Moreover, such a pessimistic account overlooks some quiet changes that are occurring in the suburbs, which may in time offer the cities relief. The suburbs are changing; they are gradually becoming more urbanized.

These changes may alleviate the racial bipolarization of cities and suburbs now so evident. For a variety of reasons, and despite efforts to prevent this, one might expect that by the century's end the suburbs will be on the way to having their full share of poor people, older citizens, and racial minorities. Such a development will go a long way toward eliminating the startling socioeconomic differences between city and suburb that presently exist, but it also will alter the existing character of the suburb that many find desirable.

The suburbs are already well advanced along the road to urbanization. The prototypical suburb is usually considered to be the "picturesque" upper-middle-class residential suburb that I have considered characteristic of phase one of suburbanization. Yet suburbs have always contained other types of communities. Many of these were existing large towns close by the city that fell into the area of metropolitan expansion and hence already contain some elements of a lower or working class and minority population. As these communities age they have begun to resemble both physically and socially the neighborhoods of the central city just over the border.

But it is in the tract developments built since World War II that we can best examine the changes in suburbia that are representative of phase two. The view of the suburbs as a place where husbands commute from work in the city to a mortgaged house surrounded by a yard is increasingly obsolete. For one thing, most of the work force no longer commutes to the city. Our larger suburbs now report as much as 70 to 80 per cent of their working people are already employed within their own borders. Suburban governments frequently want to encourage industrial and commercial developments, but are concerned about their effects on the residential life, which is what originally attracted people to their communities.

Until the mid-sixties, the single-family house remained the paramount feature of the suburbs, a visible expression of a continuing commitment to family-oriented communities and the American dream of home ownership. But in that decade housing costs, paced by soaring land values, rose more quickly than family incomes. From 1967 to 1973 the cost of a housing plot has risen annually by 13.4 per cent, while median-plot size has shrunk from 8,202 square feet to 6,990. By 1974 the median price of a new house was over $41,000

—beyond the means of more than two thirds of all American families.

To fill the need for less expensive forms of housing, builders and developers began to shift away from the erection of traditional detached one-family homes to the construction of apartment buildings of varying heights and cluster housing which use party walls between units. At the present time less than half of all new building is single-family detached. Many housing experts predict that the trend away from the traditional single-family house will continue at an accelerating rate. Yet it was this type of housing built six or less to the acre that was the basic building block of the suburbs.

The ubiquitous presence of the single-family house standing on its own lot explained the low density of the suburb as well as its middle-class and family-oriented character. As suburbs develop a mixed-housing stock, resembling cities in this regard, they must become socially more heterogeneous. In all probability they will cease to be areas populated predominantly by families with children.

Already two groups formerly thought of as belonging in the city—unmarried individuals and childless couples—are increasingly found in the suburbs. The movement to the city of empty-nesters, suburban parents whose children have left home, predicted in the 1950s has not materialized. Instead developers have built various types of suburban retirement villages with golf courses and community centers, but with children under eighteen usually not permitted. On the other hand, the "singles' bar" has become almost as commonplace a part of suburbia as the drive-in fast-food chain. Builders, especially in California, prepare special "amenity housing packages" for the singles group, too. Although the suburbs are acquiring a full range of life stages, this tendency toward specialized housing oriented toward various age levels is troubling to those who would prefer to see all groups integrated spatially and socially into a single community.

For the poor, however—and in the United States this includes a disproportionate representation of minorities—one cannot expect builders to provide "amenity packages," or even basic housing. Their housing wants really cannot be met anywhere by the private market, but especially not in the suburbs. Only public housing can meet their needs, and allow them entry into the suburbs in significant numbers. Yet most suburban communities have proved reluctant to accept more than token public housing, and even this is usually reserved for those already in the community.

As the suburbs increase in population and diversity, there are many who fear such changes threaten the suburban ideal that drew them there in the first place. Suburbanites who fled the cities do not want to see the suburbs experience urbanization. The postwar process of suburbanization, phase two, is not attractive to those who come expecting the middle-class environmental goals that were the guiding spirit of phase one. Rapid change and growth, of the kind experienced since World War II, have come to be viewed as endangering the home-centered, family-oriented nature of the suburb: "the private landscape."

Many suburbs no longer want to grow. They associate increasing population with the need for expensive public services which will add to their already heavy real estate taxes, and cause the loss of open spaces through the intrusion of high-rise buildings on the low profile of their townscape. But the critics of suburban exclusiveness argue that the most compelling motive behind the actions of its proponents is the desire to avoid an influx of social undesirables, meaning, by this, lower-income groups and racial minorities.

Many suburbanites, especially those who have only recently left the cities, fear above all that the racial tensions and crime of the city are progressing beyond the city's boundaries, and will enter their communities in the wake of the buildup. The New York *Times* recently reported on a town-zoning hearing in Suffolk County concerning the construction of luxury apartment buildings, where, "a New York City fireman leaped onto a chair, waved a newspaper full of city crime and welfare news and shouted: 'We don't want this kind of trash in our neighborhood.'"

In their efforts to ward off unwanted change, the suburbs

have armed themselves with an impressive array of weapons
that they are employing to defend their private vision: restrictive zoning, building and subdivision codes. These are used to
require single-family housing on a minimum lot size of an
acre or more, to prohibit multifamily, high-rise buildings, and
to prevent inexpensive tract development. One New York
suburban town near a college campus reacted to the movement of young people into a single-family house for the purpose of creating a commune by passing an ordinance forbidding the living together in one residence of three or more
unrelated adults. A West Coast community has already tried
to limit its population by an ordinance.

But formidable as the forces opposed to change might appear, they cannot succeed. They are under attack from civil
rights groups, land developers, and builders, and also from
federal and sometimes state and county governments. Also in
opposition to them are many of their own residents, such as
grown children, older adults, and civil servants, who are often
unable or unwilling to maintain the expensive single-family
homes demanded by exclusionary zoning. Change has been the
one constant that has always confronted the American community. And, as we have seen, suburbs are not an exception.

We also have seen that the future is elusive and difficult to
discern. Early planners were too optimistic for their time and
did not adequately take the popular vision of suburbia into
account. The pessimistic view prevalent in the 1960s of a
closed suburban society and dying cities did not encompass
the amount of change that was already occurring in suburbia.
While those who live in suburban areas and hope to maintain
a certain life-style have not been fully able to resist change.

What then does the future hold in store for American suburbs? There is no adequate answer to this pressing question
but some suggestive impressions are in order. Without detailed planning and simply through drift, the suburbs may
only move further in the directions already suggested: greater
buildup, more social heterogeneity, and an ever more varied
housing stock. Single-family detached houses will be achieved

by a smaller percentage of the population, and only at much greater relative cost than today.

Decentralization of people and physical facilities from the central city will continue, with outward expansion checked only by the decreasing supply of accessible vacant land. For the era of expansive, leap-frog, splatter-dash spread of the suburbs experienced after World War II has already ended; we have entered a more restrictive stage of areal buildup. Spatial extension of suburbia, at least in the older metropolitan areas, cannot increase commensurate with expected population gains.

Population growth in already well-developed regions, then, must mean greater density in the suburbs of the future. Remaining open land will be bitterly contested for by those wanting new housing (including the building industries), and those wanting to preserve them as public recreational areas. Here and there "exclusive communities" will continue to maintain a phase-one character and appearance for those able to afford the high price tag attached to the American dream.

Still, despite increased urbanization, the suburbs will retain their centerless, spread character. Most service facilities, including public ones, and perhaps even schools, will be found in giant freestanding multiuse malls. These will be the new civic and cultural as well as commercial centers, all but making obsolete main street and strip shopping. Covered to guard against inclement weather, representing the latest in technological advances and architectural fancies, they will be conveniently located at the nexus of expressway systems. Serving vast areas on the basis of convenience and accessibility only, such centers will further erode the already weak sense of local and community identity. By and large, the future suburbs might be as Daniel Boorstein has already found them: "a world of brand names . . . of franchised outlets and of repeatable experiences."

One can, however, offer alternative scenarios for the future. Among those who have been critical of postwar suburban spread, no group has been more outspoken than the planners. Allowed little significant role in suburban growth to date, they are dissatisfied with existing developments and concerned with what these presage. In particular many planners disapprove of the waste of resources, especially open space, entailed by suburban spread, and unnecessary low density; they are also critical of the absence of public transportation and the need for an almost total reliance on the private automobile with its consequences for pollution.

Planners also believe that suburbs require core areas offering commercial, civic, and cultural activities placed centrally to provide an anchor for communities, a focus for assemblage, and that this need cannot be met by the multiuse regional malls described earlier. Beyond this, however, planners view the present suburbs as too selective and segregated and find that they fail to offer adequate individual choice in housing and life-style.

As did Ebenezer Howard over seventy years ago, planners now argue that there is need for long-range concepts of where and how communities should develop. Behind this assumption is an underlying faith that the construction of effective mass transit systems, carefully co-ordinated to well designed land-use plans, might achieve orderly and satisfying suburban development. To further this goal of long-range controlled growth directed into planned communities, several metropolitan areas in the 1960s adopted regional master plans.

The most celebrated, and indeed comprehensive, example of such schemes was the Washington, D.C., area's "A Policy Plan for the Year 2000." First issued in 1961 it has been modified in detail several times since. This plan accepted the inevitability of continuing formless sprawl for the immediate future, but in time it hoped to concentrate buildup along main corridors of radial travel. To do this the plan called for the building of a mass transit system radiating outward along six routes from the downtown area of Washington, like spokes of a wheel. Outlying stations were to be spaced four to six miles apart as nodes around which to develop new towns. Wedges of open space in the interstices between the radial corridors were to be retained for rural or recreational use when possible. The resulting pattern of development would produce a starlike configuration set off by the wedges of open space between the urban extensions—somewhat like a hand with its fingers extended.

Washington, D.C., and the surrounding counties in two states have committed themselves to this plan, but tangible results have been disappointing. Most importantly, the rapid transportation system remains undone. In its absence, spread development of the metropolitan area has continued. Land intended for "wedge" areas has proven difficult to acquire, and some of this proposed open space is already experiencing suburban-spread buildup.

In 1969 the National Committee on Urban Growth Policy urged the construction of new towns as the key to a rational ordering of future suburban expansion. They cited, as examples of what might be done, the new town planning policy followed by Britain and the Scandinavian nations since World War II. Essentially, a new town is a form of urban development designed and developed as a unified concept. It must be of sufficient scale—though population can vary from 25,000 to 250,000—to provide residents a substantial range of essential land uses and public services as well as considerable employment opportunities.

New towns offer a distinct contrast to spread suburbs. The planners' intent in new towns usually is to create a framework of an identifiable community to which people of varying incomes, value styles, and life stages can relate effectively. Most American new town plans, following the British model, rely on a "town center concept." This center acts as a focus for business and civic activity, around which are grouped multifamily apartments and town houses in fairly high density to provide both a variety of housing styles and an urban nucleus for the community. Farther away from the center would be cluster and detached houses at a somewhat lower level of density (though still higher than the usual American suburban standards) and organized into neighborhood units with their own social centers and convenience shopping. As much open land as possible is retained for public use, while organized for convenient access. The resulting community, then, would be fairly compact, centered about a core, pedestrian-oriented, planned for efficiency and convenience, and would function as a complete and supportive community.

The federal government has authorized a program of mortgaged insurance to aid and encourage the development of new towns. Through this law, Title VII of the Housing and Development Act of 1970, Congress hoped to promote innovative, racially and economically integrated, planned communities on the fringe of large metropolitan areas. By 1975 there were fifteen new communities underway with financing of over $300 million in federally guaranteed bonds under the 1970 law, and about a dozen more being built without direct federal assistance. Hard hit by the economic crisis of the last several years, most are experiencing serious financial difficulties and falling behind in development schedules. At present a debate is underway in the Department of Housing and Urban Development on whether to continue the program, and indeed whether new towns represent a viable alternative to the erratic suburban sprawl we have been experiencing.

But as we have seen, the future is not determined solely by planning or drift. Unexpected events contribute a mighty force for change and the most important one now seems to be the energy crisis. The modern suburb must be viewed as a consequence of the affluence created in the nineteenth century by the industrial revolution. As wealth became more general and dispersed in the twentieth century, elements of the population, other than the wealthy, were permitted the choice of living in suburbia. There is now evidence that after two centuries of rapacious use of limited natural resources we are entering a new era which will require sparser, leaner living.

If this becomes fact, our present suburbs must be challenged as wasteful. A study by the Regional Plan Association has shown that suburban dwellers use one third more energy per capita than do urban dwellers. Other studies have demonstrated that suburban tracts of between one and four families per acre cost more in municipal service than their taxes return. Only at a level of four or more families per acre does each household begin to pay its own way. Above all, our sprawl suburbs must be accused of encouraging the promiscuous use of the private automobile (as evidenced by the need for two cars per family) at a time when ecological and economic imperatives demand a dramatic reduction in reliance on this energy-draining chariot.

America already appears heading for fundamental economic dislocations, and these may not be temporary but permanent. The prospect is for a major reduction in the standard of living, and this in turn will bring about pressure for the reorganization of our communities. In such an event, it would seem inevitable that not only the sprawl suburbs of phase two, but the private vision of phase one would necessarily become obsolete. To take their place would be a national program of population distribution similar to the ones urged by Howard in the 1890s and the regional planners of the 1960s.

It has become apparent that the enrichment of the "private landscape" came at great cost to our public space and communal life. As an environmental concept its roots are found in a sense of disjunction between the world of the family and the larger society. But the model of the nineteenth-century nuclear family with which this essay began is also undergoing change. Women are having fewer children and having them earlier, and this combined with women's liberation has encouraged more of them to take jobs and follow careers. At the same time, a tendency has become manifested to redefine work to allow greater time and energy for recreation and personal development. The family of carefully specialized function may be disappearing, and with this the stress on home-centeredness will weaken. There will be greater pressure for the planner to provide models of an environment that emphasizes public space and facilitates the development of collective services. Communities would then be designed in terms of such priorities as the conservation of resources and the provision of services.

As America is entering the last quarter of the twentieth century it faces an unsettling period of adjustment, probably greater than ever confronted in the past. Our spread suburbs as a creature of a profligate society may well fall victim to these changes. Social change on a vast scale is often identified with conflict. The type of changes this country confronts of decreasing national wealth and lowering of individual income seems particularly fraught with danger. Yet both national wealth and individual income are abstract concepts arrived at through using various quantifiable measures of economic activity. They do not necessarily bear correlation to the quality of life and the changing needs of individuals or social units. Our suburbs have not really proven satisfactory. The economic crisis combined with new social expectations may force us to adopt regional planning of the type described for the Washington area. Our future suburbs, then, could provide for satisfactory communities, offering more, not less, choices and services than enjoyed now.

BIBLIOGRAPHY

ASIDE FROM BELLAMY's novels and Howard's *Garden Cities of Tomorrow* (Cambridge, Mass., 1965) a fascinating instance of turn-of-the-century exercises in prognostication is H. G. Wells, *Anticipations* (London, 1902) which predicted and celebrated the twentieth-century trend toward population dispersal. In his suspicion of technology and strong emphasis on humanistic values, Lewis Mumford in "Suburbia and Beyond," 482–524 in *The City in History* (New York, 1961), offers striking contrast to Wells's optimism. A provocative effort at projecting a future community oriented away from consumption and the private landscape is Percival and Paul Goodman, *Communitas* (Chicago, 1947).

Two excellent readers on contemporary suburbia and its problems are Charles M. Haar, *The End of Innocence* (Glenview, Ill., 1972) and Louis H. Massotti and Jeffrey K. Hadden, *The Urbanization of the Suburbs* (Beverly Hills, Calif., 1973). The latter contains an exhaustive and most useful bibliography on the subject. Herbert Gans, *The Levittowners: Ways of Life and Politics in a New Suburban*

Community (New York, 1967) is the best study of an American suburb, dispassionate and perceptive. William H. Whyte, Jr., *The Organization Man* (New York, 1956) develops an acerbic analysis of the middle-class residential suburb of Park Forest, Illinois.

Mel Scott's *American City Planning Since 1890* (Berkeley, Calif., 1969) is a comprehensive, highly detailed study of the subject, and the reader is advised to approach it with specific interests in mind. *How to Save Urban America,* prepared by the Regional Plan Association, is a clear, concise, albeit somewhat simplistic, presentation of the problems that are the concern of regional planning. In recent years a considerable literature has developed on new towns, both in the United States and elsewhere. Most of this has been written by proponents of a federal new town program. Among the more interesting are Donald Canty ed., *The New City: A Program for Nationalization Urbanization Strategy* (New York, 1969) and James Bailey ed., *New Towns in America,* published by the American Institute of Architects (1973). Gurney Breckenfeld in *Columbia and the New Cities* (New York, 1971) has given us an account of America's best-known new town. An overall treatment of planned communities throughout the world is provided by two staunch supporters of Howard's garden city approach in F. J. Osborn and Arnold Whittick *New Towns* (New York, 1971).

An effort to project the future, as well as a program to shape it, is the Advisory Commission on Intergovernmental Relations' *Urban and Rural America: Policies for Future Growth* (Washington, D.C., 1968). Dennis Sobin's *The Future of the American Suburbs* (Port Washington, N.Y., 1971), despite its title, is essentially based on Nassau and Suffolk counties of New York. Two works by eminent geographers and demographers might usefully be consulted in terms of population movement and growth and their effects on settlement patterns. These are Brian J. L. Berry, "The Geography of the United States in the Year 2000," *Transactions of the Institute of British Geographers,* 51 (1970), 283–303; and P. L. Hodge and Philip M. Hauser, *The*

Challenge of America's Metropolitan Population Outlook, (New York, 1968). Trends in housing are briefly treated in George S. Sternlieb's "Death of the American Dream House," *Society,* 9 (February, 1972), 39–42. D. L. Birch, *The Economic Future of City and Suburb,* published by the Committee for Economic Development (New York, 1970), is well worth reading. The implications of continuing urban spread on resources based on 1970 census findings is handled in *Growth and Settlement in the U.S.: Past Trends and Future Issues* (1975) prepared by the Regional Plan Association.

INDEX